How to Implement a

SUCCESSFUL PROCUREMENT SYSTEM

Implement a procurement system with a simple, 5-step process

NADEEM SURVE

Orders: Please contact Nadeem Surve

You can also order via the e mail address
Nadeem.Surve1@gmail.com

ISBN: 978-0-9955997-0-3

First published 2017

Printed in Great Britain for Nadeem Surve by Bell & Bain Ltd, 303 Burnfield Road, Thornliebank, Glasgow G46 7UQ

CONTENTS

FOREWORD

Foreword

Implementing a procurement system on any scale is daunting, let alone when it is in an international context in a large business, and no matter what anyone says the cloud does not make it easier...

As a technically literate Procurement Director with over 10 years working in procurement in large multinationals, often with system implementations, I can draw on my own experience in such situations, but every company / situation is different, and I am still surprised that practical material with relevant advice on the subject is hard to come by without spending large sums with external consulting organisations.

I welcome Nadeem Surve's approach to demystify the process behind such implementations and provide some real world context and experience to help you on your system journey (hopefully without making the mistakes that so many have made). Nadeem is one of those rare "techies" who can speak the language, not only of the business, but of Procurement (who let's face it can be a different breed entirely).

Of particular note are the sections on Project Implementation – set up your project for success from the beginning (and if in doubt resolve the problems now rather than later), and also the chapter on The Procurement Roadmap – mapping these processes to your company and particular set-up will be one of the most important things you do – it will expose system (and company) flaws that you need to fix – take heed of these – don't ignore them – and save yourself pain (and time) in the long run.

After all, the end objective is to save money. Whilst that can be done through negotiation with your vendors, I hope this book may help in another way - by speeding up your implementation so that you can realise the benefits in your procurement systems business case sooner.

Enjoy reading this book, and good luck with your system(s) project!

Paul Harlington:

Paul Harlington is the Procurement Director for the TUI Group, the world's number one tourism business. He joined TUI Travel PLC in 2011 at the age of 35 in 2014 was appointed as Group Procurement Director, reporting directly into the TUI Group Executive Board. Paul has previously undertaken a number of senior management roles in defence, retail and academia, mostly working in an international context. Paul holds a Master's degree in Statistics and a Bachelor's degree with Honours in Management Science. He is also a Fellow of the Chartered Institute of Procurement and Supply. In his spare time, Paul enjoys racing superbikes in a national championship.

INTRODUCTION

Introduction:

I have written this book as a procurement expert and want to share some insights on the subject based on 17 years' experience of implementing procurement processes, procurement technology and business change.

I have obtained a BSc (Hons) in Business Information Systems and obtained a 1st for my final year project based on the topic of **'An investigation to distinguish whether project management influences Project failures'**

The aim of the book is to understand the challenges that businesses will face during the implementation of a procurement system on an international level and, by reading this book, reduce the complexity and risks involved to ensure success.

As a procurement professional, I have worked for all of the Big 4 Consultancies as well as several end user clients to help implement procurement processes and systems. I have experience in lots of different roles on projects from Business Analyst, Architect to Consultant, Technical / Functional and Training & Development.

I have worked across many industries including:

- Logistics
- Travel & Tourism
- Pharmaceuticals / Retail
- Local Government
- Travel
- Manufacturing

The book is primarily aimed at consultants, senior management, stakeholders, procurement professionals, business analysts and anyone who has an objective to learn about procurement.

The book will cover the following areas:

- Top 10 Tips for a Successful International Procurement System
- Key Procurement Strategies (Source to Pay Processes)
- Project Strategies
- The Technology Elements
- The importance of Change Management

I am available to help share knowledge, give consulting advice or deliver workshops and can be contacted as detailed below:

LinkedIn: https://uk.linkedin.com/in/nadeem-surve-28b61a2
Email: Nadeem.Surve1@gmail.com
Telephone: 07870 570 120

Facebook Author Page
https://www.facebook.com/NadeemSurveAuthor

Amazon Author Page
https://www.amazon.co.uk/-/e/B071196FL2

For management consultancy, workshops, advice, training & development, please contact Revolution Global Services Limited via email Nadeem.Surve1@gmail.com

TOP 10 TIPS

for a Successful International Procurement System

Top 10 Tips for a Successful International Procurement System

Clients typically ask for guidance on how to achieve a successful implementation of procurement as well as smooth transition to a new procurement system.

I will address this in my first chapter of the book and have listed my top ten tips below.

TIP 1 – Scope of Procurement Process

TIP 2 – The importance of Software Selection

TIP 3 – Adopt the appropriate Project Management Methods

TIP 4 – Invest in Change Management

TIP 5 – Select the right Implementation Partner

TIP 6 – Invest the right amount of time in the Planning

TIP 7 – Identify Roles and Responsibilities

TIP 8 – Communication Channels

TIP 9 – Focus on the value of Procurement and not just the Cost

TIP 10 – Collaboration

TIP 1 – Scope of Procurement Process

Procurement generally comes as part of a wider initiative to standardise finance and business processes. It is of importance to ensure that the scope of procurement is defined in order to measure the effectiveness and impact of implementing a procurement system.

I typically ask clients the following:

- What areas within procurement do you want to focus on?
- What business processes are currently causing problems for the business?

- What are your top 3 processes that require improvement?
- What are the objectives of your procurement area?
- Do you have a procurement road map?
- KPI's, Critical Success Factors, Reporting?
- What challenges do you face with your procurement strategies?

The above questions help to shape the scope of the procurement process and ensure that, once implemented; it can be measured against it.

I will discuss this in more detail in Step 1 – Procurement Strategy as well as Step 3 – Project Strategy

TIP 2 – The importance of Software Selection

Software selection is becoming more and more important nowadays as businesses start using E-Procurement tools to help automate purchasing processes.

It is always worth keeping an open mind set on what improvement means to the organisation. This also depends on the scope of procurement and the high level business requirements.

You need to be able to compare a like for like and look at the following:

- Cost of Licenses
- How easy or difficult it is to implement with finance
- Reference Site visits and feedback
- Cloud Solutions Vs. On-Premise
- Value added to procurement strategy
- Change management aspects

I will discuss this in more detail in Step 3 – Project Strategy

TIP 3 – Adopt the appropriate Project Management Methods

We are all aware of project management methodologies but, from my experience, most companies seem to either go for a very traditional approach or one which is more agile.

My advice is to look into your scope and project plan and, with the help of your implementation partner, decide on the best approach. For example, if you are only implementing a procurement system and not the complete finance package, is it really worth going for a classic waterfall methodology?

Depending on the size of change, the relevant project management methodology should be adopted.

I will discuss this in more detail in Step 3 – Project Strategy

TIP 4 – Invest in Change Management

A lot of companies have a separate change management team to manage the transition from old to new. I have found from previous experience that change management requires specific attention and should be given some importance. Taking time to ensure the change management team fully understand the gaps, changes and new processes will benefit the procurement system and also the business.

I find that using the below medium helps with the process:

- Process Walkthroughs
- Solution Design Workshops
- Roadshows
- Newsletters

I will discuss this in more detail in Step 5 – Change Management

TIP 5 – Select the right Implementation Partner

From my experience, I have worked for many implementation partners across various industries. They all have their own unique selling points and some are more experienced than others.

Most businesses determine the implementation partner based on cost, experience, previous engagement and delivery of implementation. Businesses also look at track history and follow-up with reference site visits to verify the performance of implementation partners.

It is highly recommended that background checks are performed before choosing an implementation partner. In most cases, I would follow a tendering process and invite 3 implementation partners to battle for the project.

Setting up clear guidelines and criteria makes the process a lot easier.

I will discuss this in more detail in Step 3 – Project Strategy as well as Step 4 – Project Life Cycle

TIP 6 – Invest the right amount of time in the Planning

I have worked on many projects where the planning was done to the most detail level and due to project demands, unforeseen circumstances; the planning had to be re-planned. This led to a loss of time on the project and had a knock on impact on implementing a procurement system.

It is important to spend the right amount of time on planning upfront and then revisiting specific areas rather than having to rewrite the complete plan. The plan should start as high level and, based on the project methodology, the detail should be populated by leads from each work streams. This topic will be discussed in more detail in a later chapter.

I will discuss this in more detail in Step 3 – Project Strategy

TIP 7 – Identify Roles and Responsibilities

One area that always seems to confuse many people is their role within a project, especially when it comes to procurement projects.

I have worked on small projects where it has just been me as the consultant, an implementation partner and a business representative (Subject Matter Expert). On large projects, the business roles including the SME's, business representatives and business analysts are not always well defined.

It benefits success of a procurement system, if the business representatives are identified and understand their role in the process.

I will discuss this in more detail in Step 3 – Project Strategy

TIP 8 – Communication Channels

Companies should invest and agree on the appropriate communication methods to be used as early as possible. I have observed many organisations where they have open communication channels but information gets leaked and is not communicated correctly.

There is a fine line between too much and not enough communication and the balance is an important factor. Transparency is very important when implementing procurement systems because without it, you may end up incorrectly building a solution that works for you and not for others.

I will discuss this in more detail in Step 5 – Change Management

TIP 9 – Focus on the value of Procurement and not just the Cost

A lot of companies that I have worked with generally look at cost reductions instead of focusing on what value procurement can bring to the organisation. The general rule is, if you can do more business with suppliers that you currently do business with and set up contracts with them, you are more likely to get a better level of service and discounts. It also builds better relationships with the suppliers.

Most of the organisations that I have visited do not seem to have a lot of contracts in place with suppliers. This makes reporting on spend very challenging.

I would encourage organisations to focus on getting the source to award process defined, with a very strong procurement roadmap based on a procurement strategy. This will help ensure purchasing and value is being added during the complete source to pay process.

I will discuss this in more detail in Step 2 – Procurement Roadmap

TIP 10 – Collaboration

Over the last 15 years, technology has excelled to a level where collaboration is made easy. However, even in today's world, I find organisations do not collaborate effectively within a project environment when implementing procurement and finance systems. They seem to work in little groups and only when you come to the detail, you realise there are still gaps. By then it is too late and the project risks delays to fix this integration.

Collaboration and integration is crucial between the project and business work streams to ensure the success of implementing a procurement system. This topic will be discussed in more detail in a later chapter.

I will discuss this in more detail in Step 3 – Project Strategy

Summary:

To deliver source to pay (S2P) excellence, organisations need to have a clear defined scope and value. Procurement strategies are complex but need clear direction from the procurement director to help shape the corporate strategy. Metrics should be in place manage effectiveness and to measure performance against project strategies.

The above tips should be applied to ensure that your procurement processes and systems are implemented with very little risk and with a better chance of success.

STEP 1

PROCUREMENT STRATEGY

STEP 1 – Procurement Strategy

Summary of Step 1:

As the world of procurement is rapidly changing, it is important that the procurement strategy also has the vision and capabilities to evolve. It must take into account organisation, processes and technology along with ensuring it fulfils the corporate goals set by the organisation.

Finally, the procurement strategy should be systematic, look at the long term goals and take on a holistic approach to ensure it stays ahead of the market.

The world of procurement is ever evolving and procurement is no longer passive in the corporate world. In the 1970's procurement was viewed as an administrative function but my experience demonstrates, that organisations have realised that it is less administrative and more strategic.

Since the introduction of technology along with the internet, this has impacted people, processes and has helped to make procurement more strategic. This has also led to changing how organisations view procurement and, in particular, the strategies adopted on group, regional or country level.

The starting point of the procurement process is the development of a Procurement Strategy. A procurement strategy is often referred to as a planned approach of cost effectively purchasing goods / services by implementing streamlined process and by collaborating with suppliers. This includes taking into consideration several elements and factors such as supplier enablement, the timeline for procurement, the financials including funding and budget, the projected risks and opportunities, among others.

This chapter addresses some of the key points around procurement strategies. Developing a best practice procurement strategy can be very complex based on the size of the business and the corporate objectives set by finance.

In recent years, organisations have realised that procurement plays a key role to the overall success of the companies' objectives and they understand that procurement has a direct link to the profitability of the organisations. In the past, finance has looked at procurement as a small contributor to their success and in some cases purchase on behalf of the business.

There is plenty of literature on how to build a successful procurement strategy but I am looking at the key components that businesses can benefit from.

From my exposure of procurement strategies, the following is important:

- Clearly defined objectives
- Category Management
- Contract Management
- Technology to support people and processes
- Streamlined / Common Design & Processes
- Reporting on gaps within the organisation
- Identify opportunities / innovative thinking
- Identify the right purchasing organisation based on organisational objectives
- Identify processes for the management of acquired smaller businesses into multinational organisations.
- How do you structure your procurement?

Procurement strategies vary depending on the type and size of the organisation, their vision and roadmap. Small organisations may deploy simple processes to manage procurement, whilst medium to large organisations may adopt procurement with innovation and automation.

To make matters complicated, different industry sectors may have different thinking processes and objectives towards procurement due to legal issues and policies that are enforced by governing bodies.

I have noticed a rising trend in large organisations acquiring (buy) smaller businesses to obtain a competitive edge and a stronger market share. The procurement strategy in this case must be flexible to allow growth in procurement within the business and for acquired businesses to changeover smoothly. This chapter will look at how businesses can changeover to the corporate procurement strategy whilst maintaining some procurement in-house.

Smaller organisations tend to start with finance or specific departments doing their own ordering, such as purchasing, receipting to invoice processing and a simplistic approach to approvals.

Large organisations benefit from deploying procurement strategies and source to award processes to help ensure that this feeds into the companies' overall objectives. Procurement processes tend to become more complex as the organisation grows and evolves, and it is essential to ensure that any changes are managed effectively.

There are several key areas that should be considered when creating a procurement strategy:

- Strong procurement leadership
- Clear procurement objectives
- Strategic sourcing with innovation
- Supplier Enablement
- Contract Management
- Robust purchasing and systems / processes
- Key Performance Measurements
- Overlap between procurement strategies and operations
- No PO no Pay initiatives
- Category Strategy & Structures
- Enablement of procurement across the organisation (acquisition strategy)

The chart below also illustrates the areas that add value to a procurement strategy:

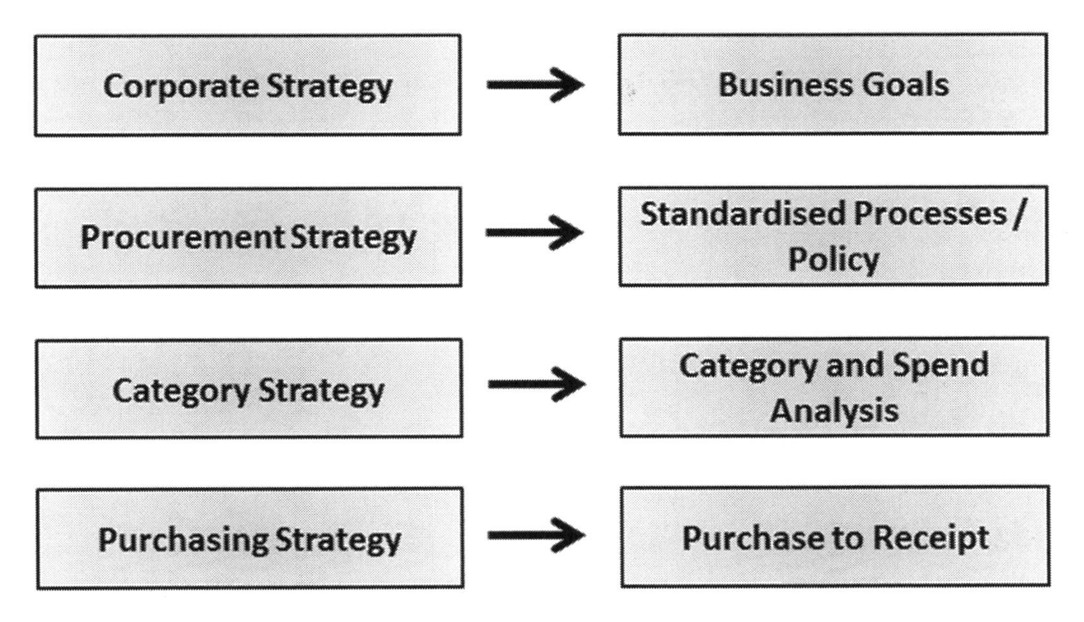

Acquiring smaller Organisations including Procurement

When large multinational organisations acquire smaller organisations to fulfil their corporate strategies, the procurement strategy should be set up to manage a pain free transition.

When deploying procurement across various business units, the heads of procurement should take into consideration the methods and tools used to implement core processes with the newly acquired business.

The transformation can happen in various ways, but can be challenging. So how can businesses be helped to transition to the new corporate way?

Let's take an example where a large firm takes over another business. From a corporate strategic perspective, the newly acquired business should be reviewed in terms of its current practices and processes from the business side and take into account any good practices that could be adopted by the firm.

The procurement strategy should review and analyse current procurement strategies and identify improvements within the newly acquired business. It is always difficult to adopt common processes with people, process and technology within one organisation but, where possible, find ways to influence organisations to adhere to the procurement strategy. To this, benefits should be presented to help the transition.

As part of this, it is essential to review current corporate strategy and procurement structures including:

- Procurement Structure (People)
- Governance / Performance
- Category Management
- Purchase to Pay
- Change Management
- Technology

The goal of doing a complete review of the acquired companies' strategy is to enable change in the right direction.

Culture and environmental factors may come into play where the acquired business is not based in the same geographic location as the main firm. When trying to influence behaviours and process across all the business units, it is important not to force change too quickly.

Some organisations decide to take ownership of 80% of the strategic elements and allow the acquired company to manage local contracts. When discussing how to transition change, kick off meetings must take place, organisations should demonstrate that they are listening to feedback and when making high profile changes that impacts people, this should be communicated in a structured manner.

Indeed, I would recommend trying to always find ways to bring companies to one way of working practices and align to the procurement strategy.

The following methods can be used to achieve this:

1. Kick off sessions / Workshops
2. Process Design Walkthroughs
3. Deep dive workshops to understand processes, policies and procedures
4. Feedback and Replay sessions on analysis
5. Agreement on how to transition procurement
6. Always find ways to resolve dispute and listen to both sides

Some organisations adopt a decentralised model where they realise that the acquired company would not add value to joining the procurement strategy, because the overheads to add them to the strategy are too high, as a result leave them as decentralised.

There must be mutual benefit to bring organisations on-board, but the analysis must demonstrate that it benefits the organisation to bring them into the common strategy.

In summary, a procurement strategy must take into consideration people / organisation, technology, procurement processes and change management to identify the appropriate strategy for the organisation.

The benefit of having a procurement strategy is to bring proactive approaches to category management, analyse performance and introduce contract compliance. Also, to add value to procurement processes, automation and reduce overhead costs. A procurement strategy should be written with the corporate strategy in mind as this feeds into the main corporate strategy and objectives of the organisation.

STEP 2

PROCUREMENT ROADMAP

STEP 2 – Procurement Roadmap

Summary of Step 2:

The procurement roadmap is the next step in the process and looks at the importance of various aspects within procurement. It starts with the strategic elements, whereby suppliers are enabled via the source to award process, then discusses about how the contract award is operationally procured using the purchase to receipt processes and finally explains how suppliers are paid via the invoice processing element.

The procurement roadmap is very important to the success of procurement systems because it begins with the evaluation of vendors that could be awarded a contract based on a requirement and ends with the supplier eventually getting payment for goods and services.

The key point is to define the requirement as clearly as possible, before entering into any tendering processes. Most businesses tend to give opportunities to suppliers they currently work with to build stronger relationships and obtain better services with them.

In order to achieve the strategic and tactical goals that are set out in the procurement strategy, there are 3 procurement processes that are part of the **Source to Pay (S2P)** area.

This includes:

- **Source to Award:** This covers Spend Analytics, Strategic Sourcing and Contract Management.
- **Spend Analytics:** Analysis of spend, identify cost saving initiatives, decision making, support contract management
- **Strategic Sourcing:** Following the above theme, based on the analysis of spend to demonstrate potential improvements, new supplier enablement and tendering processes.

- **Contract Management:** Award contracts to successful bidders based on the tendering process and manage the contracts going forward into the operational area of procurement.

The process begins with requirements that may need to go through a tender process or analysis of supplier performance and spend. Large organisations that have strategic procurement initiatives would deploy Source to Award processes.

- **Purchase to Receipt:** This covers Requisitioning, PO Creation and Goods Receipting.
  - **Requisitioning**: The ability to request a PO and follow internal approvals for financial and purchasing budgets.
  - **PO Creation**: Legal documents sent to vendors for goods / services.
  - **Goods Receipts**: Confirmation for the requester of the PO that goods have been received and services provided.

This process includes the operational purchasing processes and includes the creation of purchase requests that leads into purchase orders (PO's). The purchase to receipt processes has very strong financial integration along with implications and relies upon financial data for accruals and committed spend.

- **Invoice Processing**: This business process focuses on matching invoices to PO's via receipts and making payment to the supplier.
  - **2 Way Match Process**: Match an invoice against a PO directly without the need for goods receipts.
  - **3 Way Match Process**: Match an invoice against a PO directly with the need for goods receipts.
  - **Self-Billing**: When a Goods Receipt is created against a PO, an invoice is automatically created and paid.
  - **Financial Invoice**: This is where no PO exists and the procurement strategy has identified a non-PO process for specific types of spending. Invoices are sent for approval and then paid.

The diagram below illustrates the main areas covered as part the procurement roadmap:

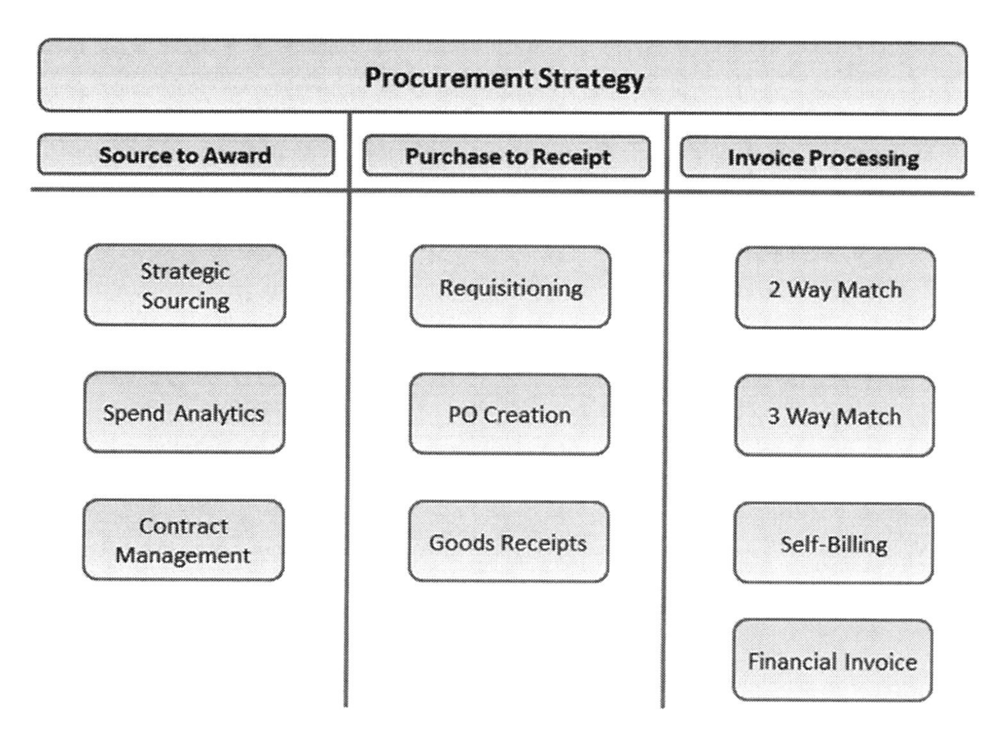

Now that the main areas of the roadmap have been explained, let's discuss the individual steps within each sub area.

The below roadmap demonstrates the high level summary of the Source to Pay processes and how they interlink with each other:

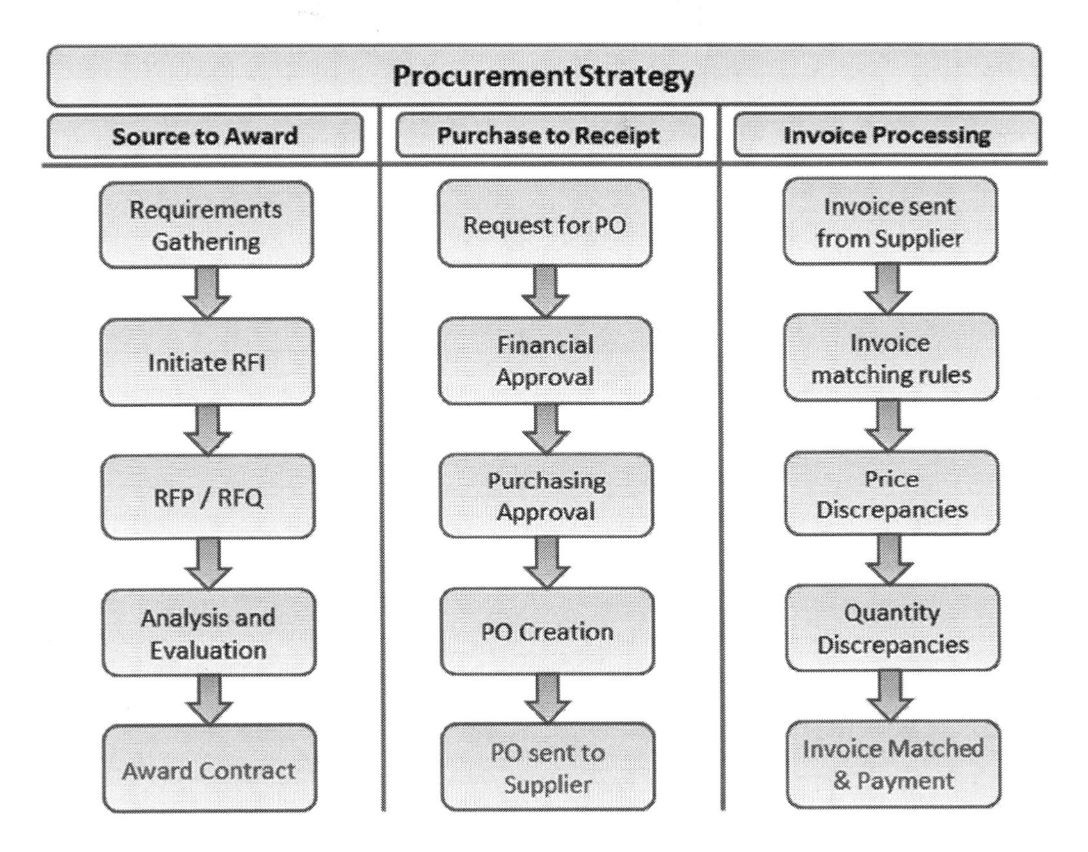

1. Source to Award

This section will discuss each of the steps involved in the **Source to Award Process**. As demonstrated in the Source to Pay Roadmap above, the process starts with a requirement that needs to be fulfilled. There are various people that are involved within the Source to Award Process.

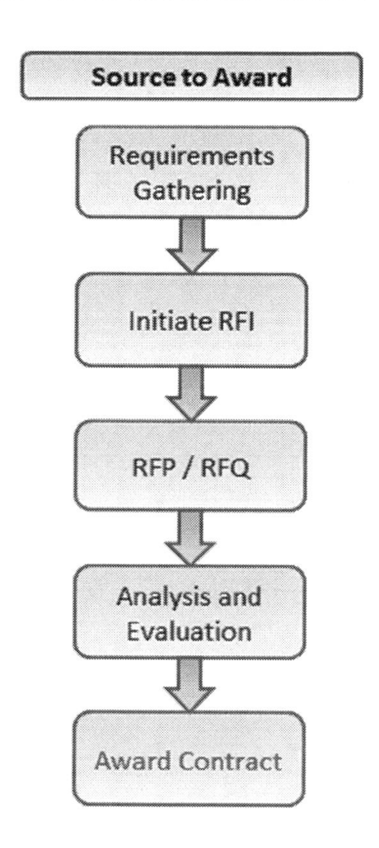

Typically, the Source to Award process is adopted based on the procurement strategy and the type of the requirement. In some cases, it could start 18 months before a vendor contract is up for renewal or when a new project is about to kick off. It could last from 1 to 12 months.

From experience, organisations try and ensure this process is less painful and complicated by developing a procurement strategy which is aligned to the business and financial strategy. Also, sometimes a project team is in place to complete the feasibility or investigatory components to set out the requirements.

If the source to award process is not effectively managed, it can affect the overall procurement strategy and have legal and financial implications for the organisation. A badly managed and incorrectly defined requirement can impact the organisations established reputation and capability of delivering goods / services to its customers.

For example, if there was a tender for a new network to be installed at your workplace and the requirements were not identified and documented accurately, this could have an impact on what is physically delivered and users may not be able to function, leading to service outages. There could be security risks, outages due to bandwidth and loss of connectivity.

Also, flexibility and innovation is important to this process. Thinking outside of the box can bring competitive advantage as each organisation looks to find ways to do procurement smartly and more effectively. Each process step has a clearly defined start and end point.

The chart below illustrates a detailed Source to Award Process:

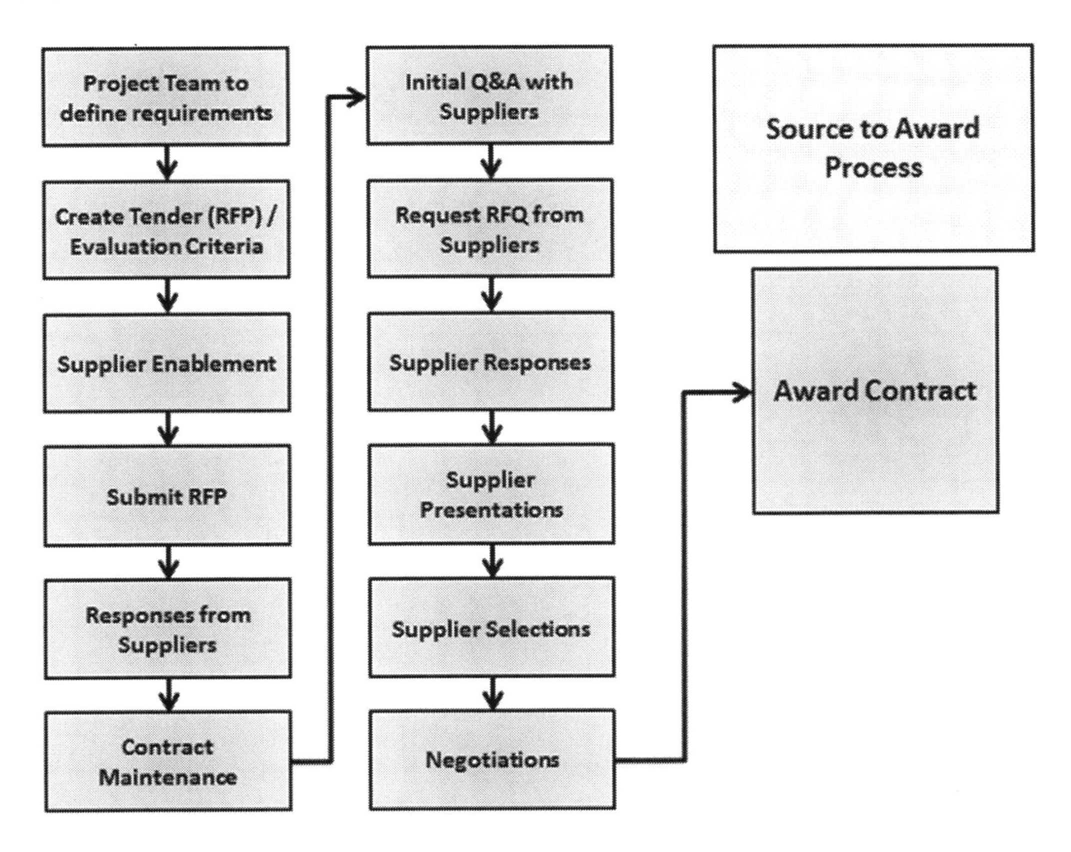

As part of the requirements gathering step, organisations may invest in developing a project team to determine the requirements. For example, when upgrading current IT systems, architects and consultants will investigate various technical and software aspects and feed them into the requirements.

Based on the above detailed steps, some organisations look at innovative ways to attain the best from the vendor. They could group together some of the process steps and start discussing requirements directly with the vendor before RFP's have been submitted to understand if they are on the right track.

If organisations want to evaluate vendors, they should submit a Request for Information (RFI) to suppliers so that each has the same opportunity to respond. Ultimately, organisations tend to send RFI's / Request for Proposals (RFP's) to vendors that they currently have contracts with because these suppliers understand the organisation better.

From my exposure, the Source to Award process steps has the following types of people involved:

- **Project Team**
- **Strategic Procurement Buyer**
- **Key Stakeholders**
- **Legal Consultants**
- **Other (Specialists, Negotiators, Finance)**
- **Vendors**

The flow diagram below illustrates the main **responsibilities** that are typically completed at each stage of the Source to Award process:

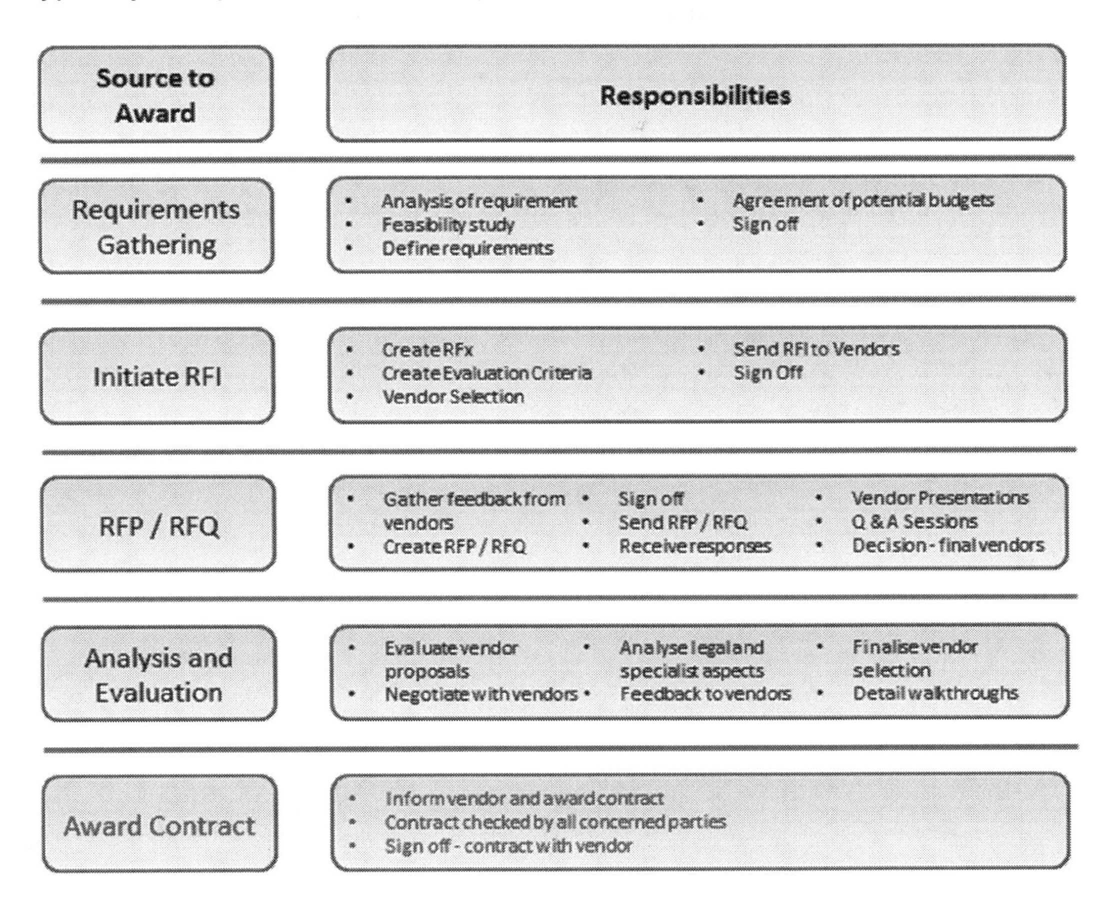

Each of the above will be discussed in more details during this chapter.

Process Step: Requirements Gathering

Requirements Gathering	• Analysis of requirement • Feasibility study • Define requirements	• Agreement of potential budgets • Sign off

The requirements gathering process step is key for the success of any tender because it identifies the requirements that will directly help achieve the organisations core objectives as well as the procurement strategy. The user (project team) must have a clear understanding of the expectations. From my experience, global organisations spend more time analysing and evaluating market trends to strategically ensure that the requirement fits into the overall objectives, as well as ensuring there are financial benefits and budgets available. Everyone wants the best products at competitive prices. It is fair to mention that price should not be the only factor during the tendering process.

Who should be involved in this step?

In the requirements gathering process, there are a few important people involved. The Project Team and Specialists start to scope out the requirements and complete the analysis and feasibility. The Strategic Procurement Buyer is in the background and approached for guidance and will analyse requirements and execute reports. The Strategic Procurement Buyer will also analyse supplier performance and evaluate purchasing trends.

The diagram below illustrates the main **roles** that are involved to complete the responsibilities:

Requirements Gathering	• End User / Stakeholder • Strategic Procurement Buyer • Architects / Specialists

End User (Project Team) / Stakeholders: This is the person(s) that understand the requirements which need to go out to tender. They also define the requirements in detail by investigating solutions.

Strategic Procurement Buyer: This person understands the procurement strategic framework and ensures that this is adhered to at all times by the project team and others. This person is also available to run procurement reports and investigate potential vendors based on requirements.

Architects / Specialists (Project Team): Depending on the requirements, Architects / Specialists such as consultants may be required to complete feasibility studies, market analysis and further investigation to define the finalised requirements.

All of the above should understand the procurement strategy and try and use them to build a strong business case. For a successful process, the objectives should be to comply by the business policies and add value to the procurement roadmap.

I have been involved in various tendering processes over the last 17 years. This has included the selection of implementation partners (services) to vendors that resell products (goods) on a global level (e.g. stationery).

- **Analysis of requirements:** The organisation should ensure that the requirements are clearly analysed against what is available in the market
- **Define requirements:** The organisation should define the requirements which helps the tendering process and vendors with their responses
- **Agree budgets:** Before taking on the analysis, clear budgets should be agreed, so that once the vendor has been awarded a contract,

there is no time wasted on budgets

- **Sign Off:** Obtain sign off from the architects, specialists based on analysis of the requirements

The diagram below illustrates **roles to responsibility** matrix. This allows an understanding of the differences within the roles during the Requirements Gathering process step:

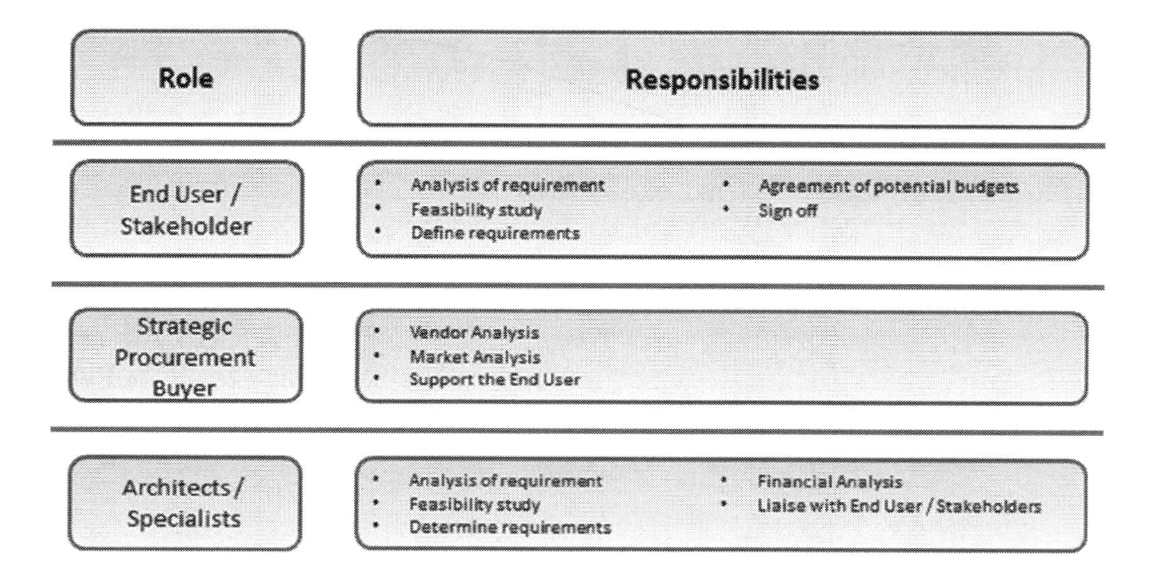

In summary, the requirements gathering process step has a number of people involved including project teams to determine the requirements, specialists to complete analysis and financial information, stakeholders to support the requirements and the strategic procurement buyer to execute reports and investigate vendor/market analysis.

It is also beneficial if the stakeholders and project teams are aware of vendors that can provide the goods / services because it helps the strategic procurement buyer during the market analysis step.

Process Step: Initiate Request for Information (Optional)

Initiate RFI

- Create RFx
- Create Evaluation Criteria
- Vendor Selection
- Send RFI to Vendors
- Sign Off

Definitions:

- A Request for Information (RFI) is used when you think you know what you want but need more information from the vendors. It will typically be followed by an RFQ or RFP (From Humboldt).
- A request for information (RFI) is a standard business process whose purpose is to collect written information about the capabilities of various suppliers. Normally it follows a format that can be used for comparative purposes (from Wikipedia).

The next process step within the source to award process is to create the Request for Information (RFI). This step is only required if you require additional information before creating the RFP from the vendor.

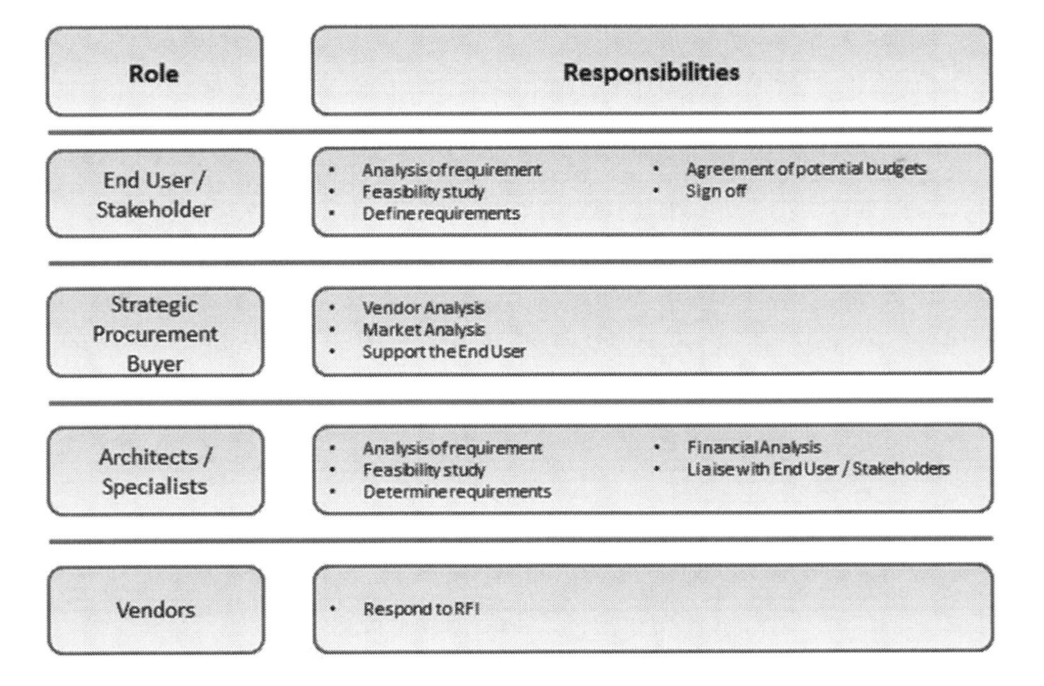

The above diagram illustrates the main **responsibilities** required during the RFI process.

Where there are gaps in the requirements an RFI can be sent to a number of vendors and responses can be added into the requirements gathering document in preparation for the RFP.

For more information and templates, contact Revolution Global Services Limited via email Nadeem.Surve1@gmail.com.

In summary, by completing the requirements gathering and RFI process, you are now ready to create the RFP / Request for Quotation (RFQ). The theory is that if the requirements have been clearly identified, the RFP should be straightforward and less time consuming. At each process step, there should be a review and sign off by the main stakeholders, strategic procurement buyer and project team. Where applicable, the procurement director may get involved in the process to ensure strategic goals are considered and met.

Process Step: Request for Proposal / Quotation

RFP / RFQ	• Gather feedback from vendors • Create RFP / RFQ	• Sign off • Send RFP / RFQ • Receive responses	• Vendor Presentations • Q & A Sessions • Decision - final vendors

Definitions:

- A request for quotation (RFQ) is a standard business process whose purpose is to invite suppliers into a bidding process to bid on specific products or services. RFQ generally means the same thing as IFB (Invitation For Bid). An RFQ typically involves more than the price per item (from Wikipedia).
- A request for proposal (RFP) is a document that solicits proposal, often made through a bidding process, by an agency or company interested in procurement of a commodity, service or valuable asset, to potential suppliers to submit business proposals (from Wikipedia)

This is a proposal document that will be sent to the supplier. If the initial process steps have been completed, the RFP should be straightforward.

The RFP document should have all the facts with clearly defined checkpoints. The evaluation criteria should also be created based on the RFP to measure the supplier responses.

The important sections that should be covered in the RFP are illustrated in the diagram below.

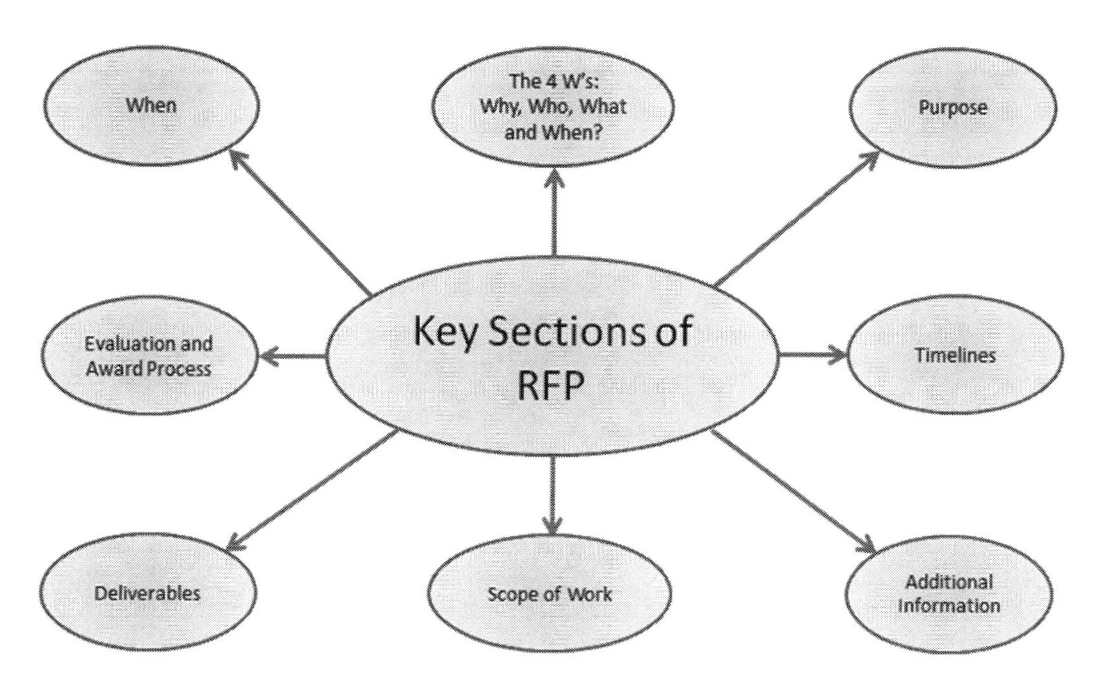

The steps are simple enough to follow as they make logical sense. The requirements gathering step should have already answered the 4 W's, the purpose, timelines, scope of work (SOW), deliverables and evaluation criteria.

Who should be involved in this step?

In the RFP process, the responsible team includes the Strategic Procurement Buyer who creates the RFP based on the requirements gathering process / RFI. The Project Team will review the RFP and sign off. In recent times, strategic buyers tend to consider vendors requested by stakeholders / project team and analyse them from a strategic perspective to ensure they meet the procurement strategy.

Organisations tend to try and do more business with vendors that already have contracts with them and along with established suppliers in the market. For example, when outsourcing software support organisations will look at support suppliers they currently work with for other support activities and analyse their capabilities. Informal workshops take place and benchmarking is completed. By doing business with vendors that you already have contracts with, the organisation is in a strong position to negotiate better discounts / services. It also allows a degree of confidence having vendors based on previous engagement or experience.

However, this is not the only way to select vendors and others may investigate into those that provide similar services.

The diagram below illustrates the main **roles** that are involved in this process:

RFP / RFQ	• End User / Stakeholder • Strategic Procurement Buyer • Architects / Specialists • Vendors

End User / Stakeholders (Project Team): Input into the RFP process with the finalised requirements. Propose potential vendors that the RFP should be submitted to. Sign off the RFP before it is sent to vendors.

Strategic Procurement Buyer: Complete the RFP, along with the evaluation criteria. Agree the submission date and the response end date. Strategically evaluate vendors and analyse the market so that the right vendors have been selected for the RFP.

Architects / Specialists: Review the RFI from the vendors and feedback on RFP document before it is submitted to vendors.

Vendors: Accept RFP / RFQ from the organisation.

The diagram below illustrates the main **responsibilities** for this process step:

RFP / RFQ	• Gather feedback from vendors • Create RFP / RFQ • Sign off • Send RFP / RFQ • Receive responses • Vendor Presentations • Q & A Sessions • Decision - final vendors

- **Create RFP:** When creating the RFP, research is the key. Defining your project as best as you can, will enable you to pass that information on to prospective vendors, but also receive proposals that are tailored to your needs by vendors who understand the requirements they are responding to. Information provided by vendors can help create a successful RFP.

- **Determine Evaluation Criteria:** Is pricing your only evaluation criteria or are you looking for the best fit and the best project for your budget? Also, if all of the companies give you proposals for roughly the same price, how will you choose your finalists? It always helps to have an evaluation criteria based on important factors. It helps the bidders tailor their responses to the RFP.

  It is important to assist the vendors with priorities and importance to you as an organisation. Good examples include speed of delivery, professional resource experience and the type of delivery method.

- **Vendor Selection:** Most organisations tend to send RFP to vendors they have relationships with or have done business with on the past.

- **Sign Off:** Obtain sign off from stakeholders, project teams, architects, specialists based on analysis of the requirements and any RFI responses from vendors.

- **Send RFP:** To receive better responses from vendors, ensure there is plenty of information in the RFP and submit to the vendors that have been agreed.

The diagram below illustrates the **role to responsibility** matrix to understand differences within the roles during the RFP process step:

Role	Responsibilities
End User / Stakeholder	• Review RFI • Evaluation criteria • Sign off • Agree vendor selection
Strategic Procurement Buyer	• Create RFP / RFQ • Create evaluation criteria • Submit RFP / RFQ to vendors
Architects / Specialists	• Review RFI • Feedback on RFP
Vendors	• Submit to vendor

In summary it is vital that all parties understand their role and responsibility throughout this process. The RFP process step involves the same people that were involved in the requirements gathering and RFI steps. The physical RFP document is created and submitted to vendors once all concerned parties have signed off. Some organisations combine the requirements gathering and RFP creation process if there is no requirement for the RFI step.

For more information and templates, contact Revolution Global Services Limited via email Nadeem.Surve1@gmail.com.

Process Step: Analysis and Evaluation

Analysis and Evaluation

- Evaluate vendor proposals
- Negotiate with vendors
- Analyse legal and specialist aspects
- Feedback to vendors
- Finalise vendor selection
- Detail walkthroughs

Definition:

Get Bids & Then Negotiate Even When Selecting a Vendor Through Tenders. You should then receive a number of bids to provide the goods or services that you are requiring. Now is the time for you to evaluate each of bids, best undertaken in a formal manner, with the intention of choosing your new vendor or vendors (from Wikipedia).

As vendors start to respond to RFP's and RFQ's, the next step of the process is to evaluate the responses based on a scoring methodology. There are various methodologies available in the market and one that has worked well for me in the past is demonstrated below:

Score Weighting Conversion

10 = Exceeds Expectations

7 = Good

5 = Satisfactory

3 = Poor

0 = Not Delivered

Results

Evaluation Criteria	Score Weighting	Company A	Company B	Company C	Company D
Supplier Profile & Financials	10	6.3	4.8	6.5	6
Accreditation & Environment	5	1.8	2.7	2.8	3.4
Service & Delivery	35	16.8	9.5	18.6	18.2
SLA	10	5.2	5.2	5.7	6.2
Cost Matrix	40	24.6	14.9	31.4	25.7
Total Score		**55**	**37**	**65**	**59**

Evaluation scores confirmed that Company C and Company D offered the best overall proposal in three key areas, Cost, Service and Capacity.

Awarding the business to one or both of the vendors would therefore be beneficial in terms of cost and services provision as well as further the organisations processes and supplier list.

The below diagram explains the main **responsibilities** involved in the Evaluation Step:

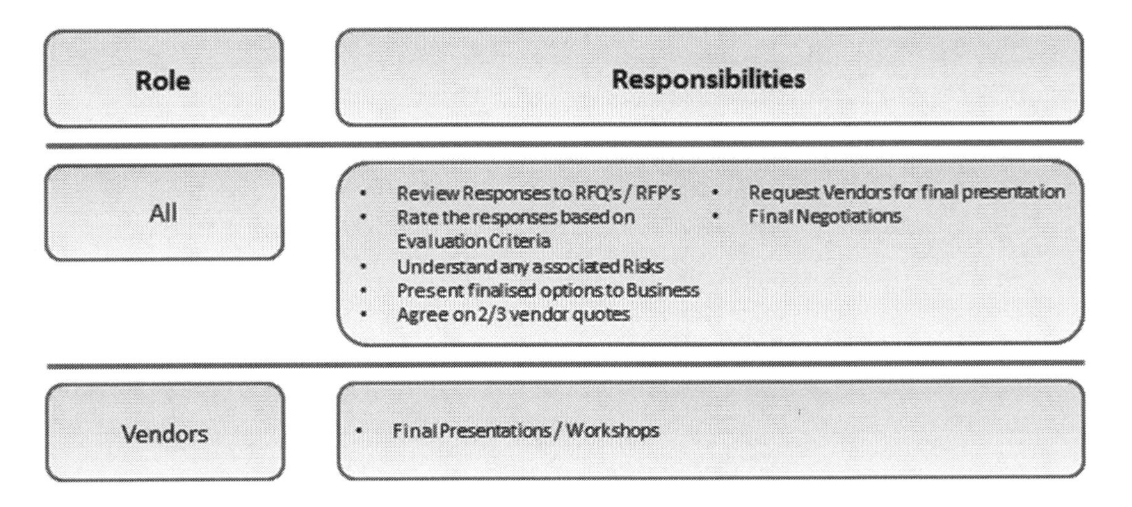

All parties need to work together to evaluate the RFP responses and then select suppliers for final RFQ's. In some organisations, RFP's and RFQ's are submitted at the same time but it can become time consuming for vendors to submit both back, so to keep it simple and separate out the documents if possible.

During the evaluation of responses from vendors, always analyse any associated risks that may cause issues in the long run against your requirements. It may benefit the organisation to hold Q&A Sessions with the vendors to mitigate any risks.

Other factors that should be considered when making the final decision on the bidder include:

- Price / cost analysis
- Smooth integration of operations into the business
- Maintain control within the business
- Stability of existing employees
- Utilisation of supplier skills

In summary, the evaluation process step is an important step which takes place post responses from vendors. Based on the evaluation criteria, the project team and strategic procurement buyer should analyse the quality of the responses, integrity of the supplier and other critical factors. Where applicable, invite suppliers to attend Q&A sessions and then make a decision based on the weightings.

Process Step: Award Contract

Award Contract

- Inform vendor and award contract
- Contract checked by all concerned parties
- Sign off - contract with vendor

Definition:

Contract awarding is the method used during a procurement in order to evaluate the proposals (tender offers) taking part and award the relevant contract. Usually at this stage the eligibility of the proposals has been concluded. So it remains to choose the most preferable among the proposed (from Wikipedia).

This is the final stage of the Source to Award process and covers the awarding of the contract to a vendor. At this stage, proposals should have been analysed and the project / strategic teams should start preparing to offer a contract. The legal department and any other bodies will be involved to finalise the contract.

An evaluation team will examine each tender received and make recommendations to the board as to which represents the best tender. A contract will be awarded based on this advice. Once the contract has been awarded, the successful and unsuccessful tenderers will be notified. Unsuccessful tenderers may obtain feedback on their performance by applying via writing.

Once the supplier has been awarded the contract, the two parties should go through the terms and conditions of the contract in detail and agree fixed rates where applicable.

Once the vendor has been chosen, contract negotiations should start and a final list of articles should be obtained from the vendor. All parties should agree on this, including legal and legislative authorities and the contract should be set up and signed by both parties.

The contract can then be handed over to the operations team to implement within the organisation. It is beneficial that the strategic procurement team explains the contract details to the operational procurement team to allow an efficient operational implementation of the contract as part of the transition.

The Operational Procurement Buyers will liaise with the supplier directly and start to implement the contract into the business. Some of the tenders that I have been involved with include grouping all stationery articles from multiple vendors into 1 supplier across the whole organisation. The supplier had a list of items which were available via a catalogue and this catalogue was made available across the UK&I and other geographical business units.

There was a technical element to implement the catalogue, but the rest of the process was very much process driven.

In summary the Award Contract step is the final step of the strategic procurement process area and this is where the contract is awarded to the winning tender and where the strategic team hand over the contract details to the operational procurement team. The transformation from strategic to operations can happen via meetings, walkthroughs and reviews with both parties and also through the introductions between the winning bidder (supplier) and the operational procurement team (business operations).

2. Purchase to Receipt

The earlier chapters explained the procurement strategy and the strategic framework to put contracts in place. This section will discuss the operational processes that are implemented to purchase and fulfil the objectives of the procurement strategy.

The purchase to receipt (requisition to receipt) process starts when there is a need to purchase goods / services. This process has a very strong integration with Finance, Master Data and Purchasing departments. Without having the relevant master data set up, employees will be unable to complete a purchase request.

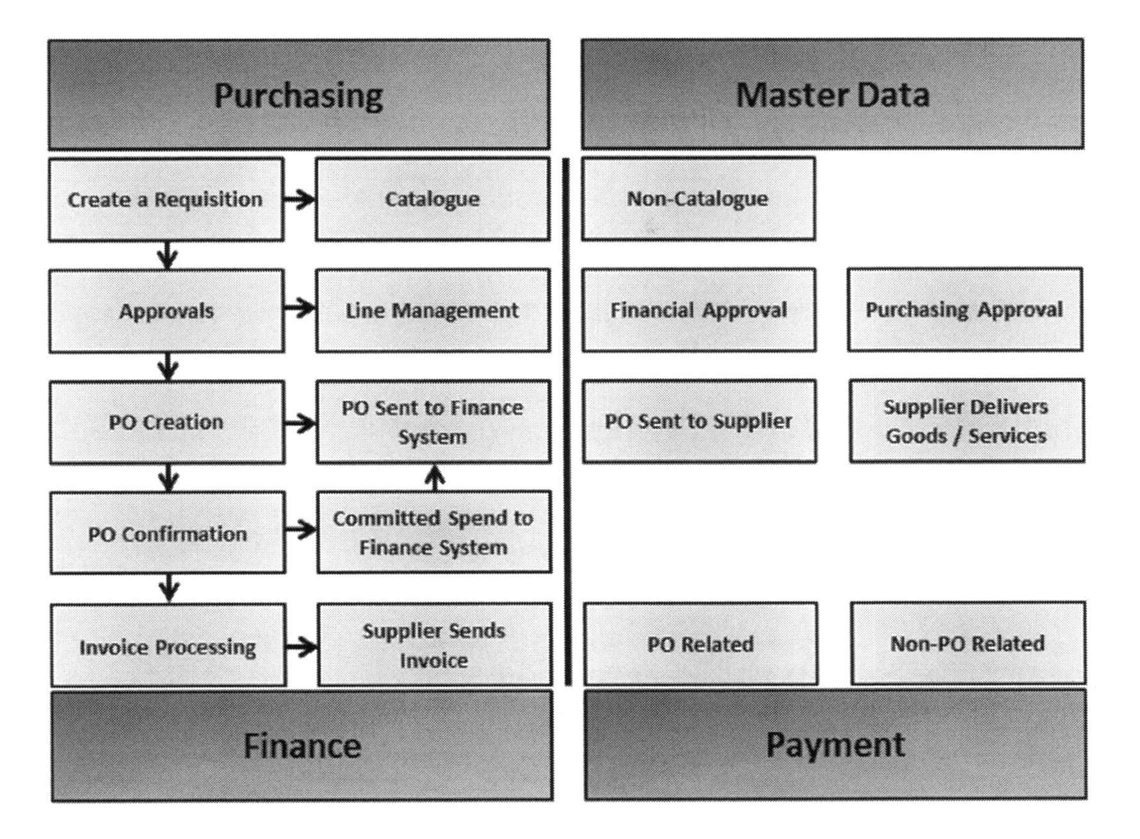

The diagram explains the main process steps that will be covered in this chapter. The purchase to receipt cycle is a standard process for both procurement professionals and suppliers alike. If you are involved in procurement at all, it is a term you may have heard thrown around, but are you aware of the actual sub processes of the cycle?

- **Realisation of Requirement**

The first part of the purchase to receipt process is the identification of requirements that need ordering. The process begins with an employee (also known as a purchase requester) who creates a purchase request and submits it to the manager. For example: an employee has realised that the department requires more printing paper, pens, pencils and writing pads so the employee will raise a purchase request and send for approval.

- **Approval of Purchase Request**

The next part of the process is the approval or rejection of the purchase request from the manager. The approval can be based on the cost, the type of request (goods / service), the product and the budget or anything else the business chooses to approve against. Authorisation is generally based on approval limits and where purchase requests exceed the managers' approval limit; it follows an approval hierarchy and sends the request to the manager in the approval chain.

I have been involved in some interesting debates around various approval models. Some approvals based on line management and others based approval line management, procurement and financials.

- **Additional Approval of Purchase Request**

After the relevant approvals have taken place, there may be some additional approvals based on departmental, specialist commodity or gatekeeper (technical approval) which come as part of the final approval step. Smaller organisations may have the same approver approving all steps, whilst larger organisations would have segregation of duty policies in place, where each approver is different.

Process flow for Additional Approval of Purchase Request is illustrated below:

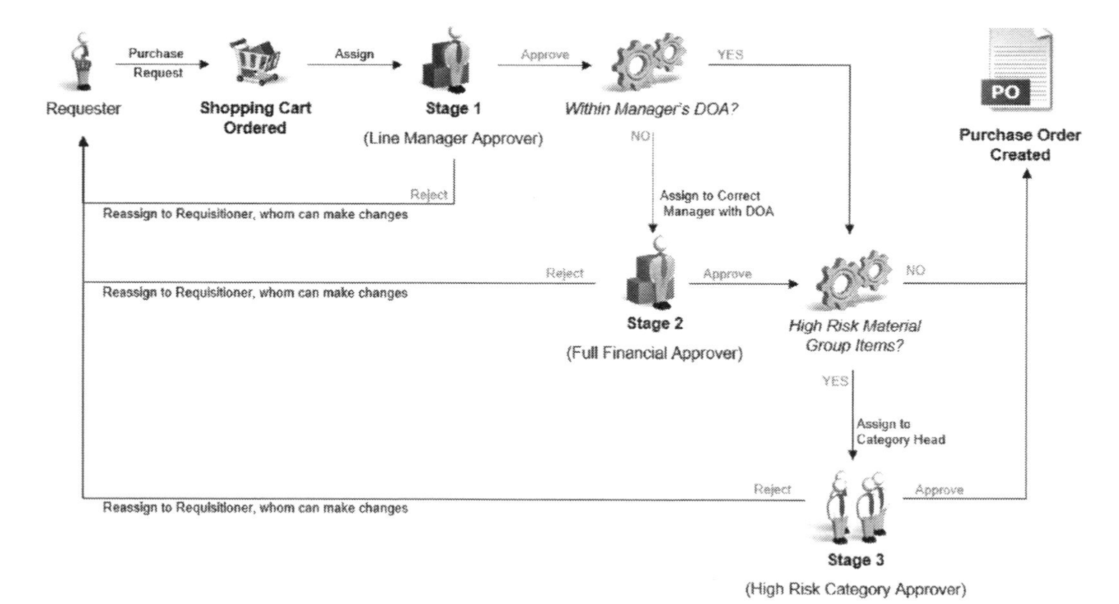

• Procurement Involvement

For non-contracted / off catalogue purchase request, the operational procurement may be required to identify any existing contracts that may exist with the supplier. If one exists, this will be created and added to the purchase request.

If a supplier contract does not exist, then the procurement function will contact the requester and identify a supplier. This supplier will be contacted for a quote and if the quote is deemed acceptable, the supplier will be set up and assigned to the request.

PO is the generated and sent to the supplier.

Process flow for Procurement Involvement is illustrated below:

Example: A

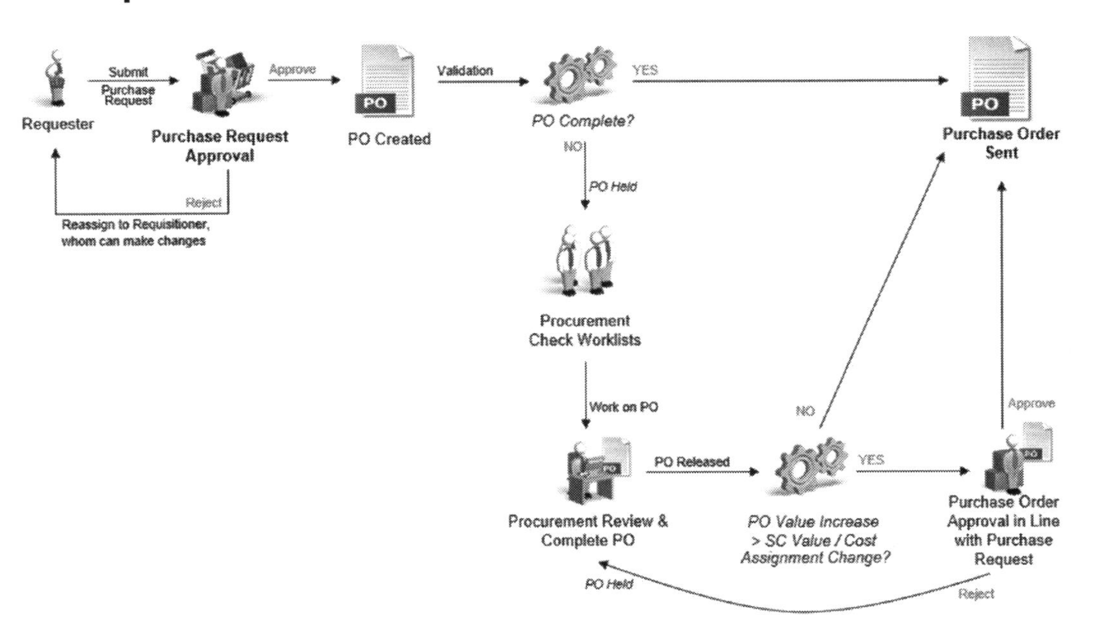

Example: B

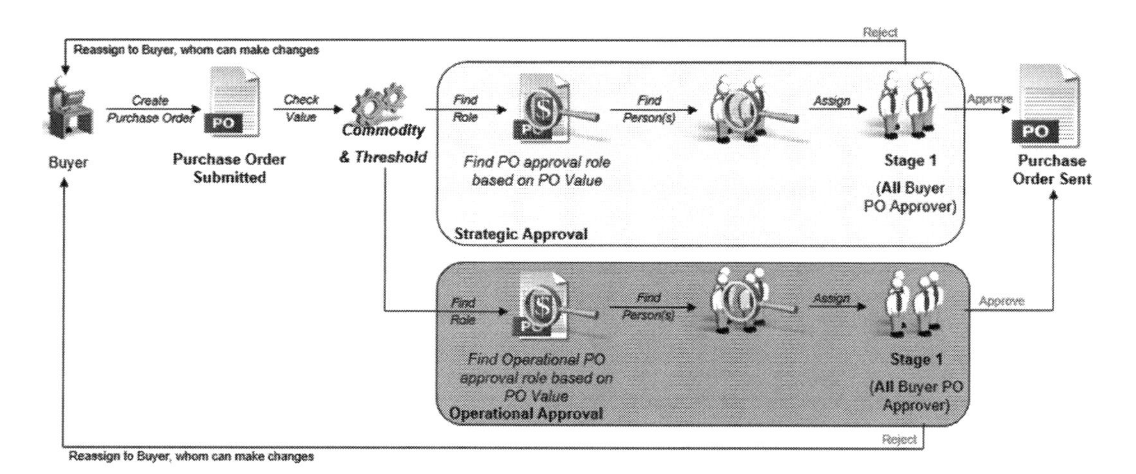

- ## Goods Receipt

When the goods are received by the organisation, the requester checks the delivery note against the PO and acknowledges the receipt. Quantity and quality are checked and any unfit items are rejected and sent back to the supplier.

Process flow for Goods Receipt is illustrated below:

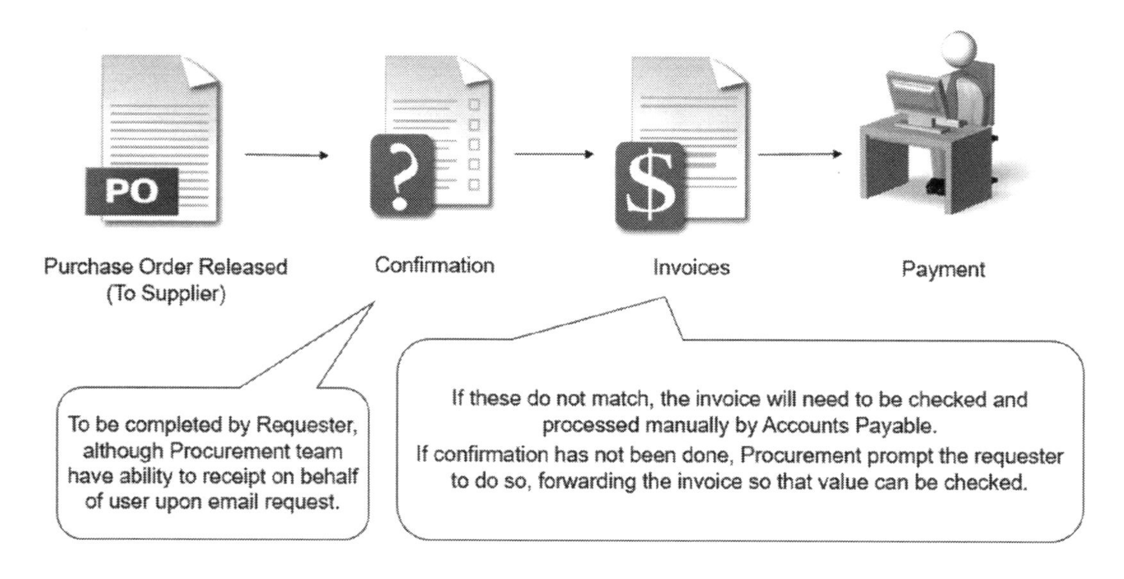

Many years ago, when basic procurement tools were implemented, employees would call suppliers directly to order or fill out a request and get it signed by the management team before ordering with the supplier (paper-based process).

Nowadays, organisations implement procurement tools and have the capability to automate approval procurement processes and to ensure budgets are signed off through approvals.

The diagram below illustrates the main **responsibilities** within each of the Purchase to Receipt process:

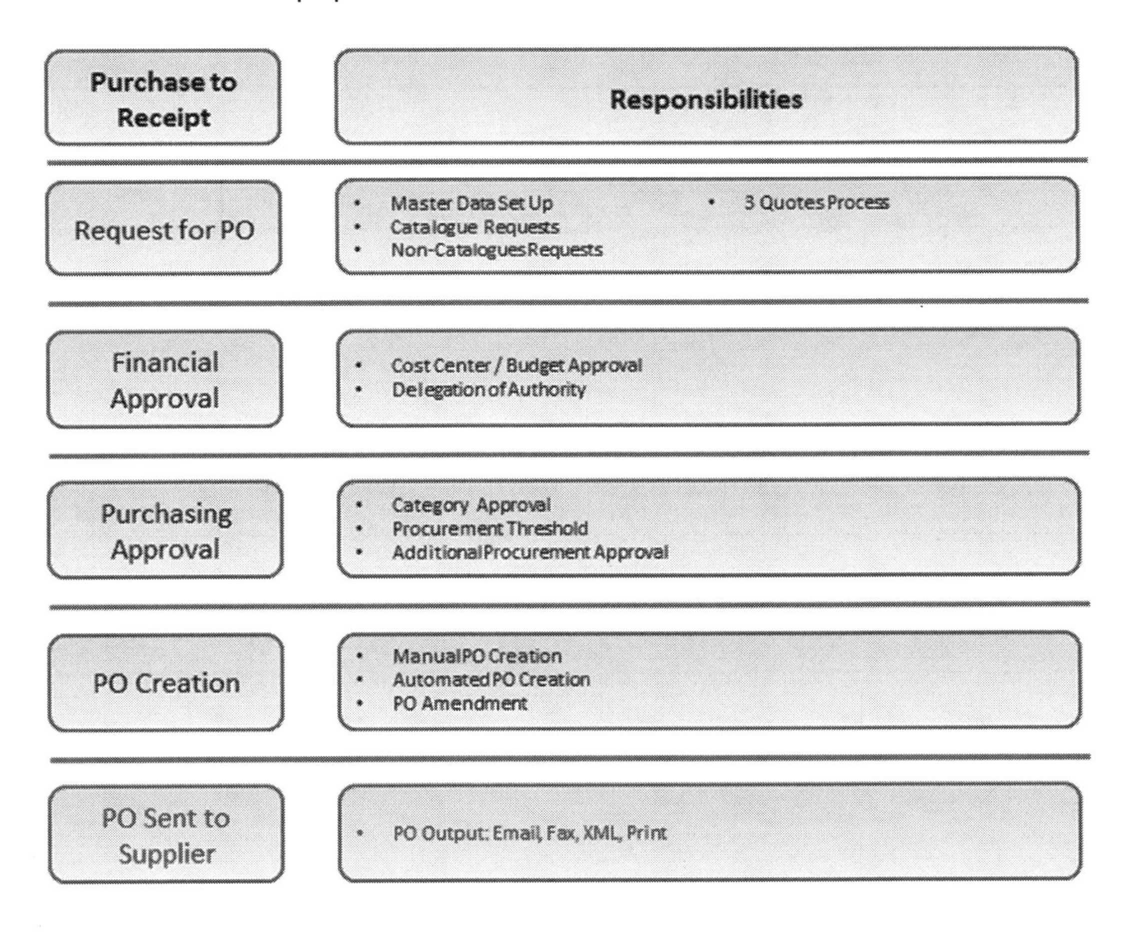

Let's now discuss each step in more detail, starting with the Request for PO process step.

Process Step: Request for Purchase Order (PO)

Request for PO

- Master Data Set Up
- Catalogue Requests
- Non-CataloguesRequests
- 3 QuotesProcess

I have worked in this area for many years and implemented various processes and systems. The start of the process is the Purchase to Receipt process and consists of the following sub areas:

- **Master Data Set Up:**

In order to request a PO, there is some master data that needs to be set up. Typical master data that should be considered includes:

- Vendors
- Finance Budget Codes
- Category (Commodity)
- Catalogues (where applicable)
- Approvers
- Delivery Addresses
- Enterprise Structure (Company Codes (legal entities))

Without the above in place, the request for PO will be difficult. The above is a contribution factor for the below processes. One area which has always been challenging is the category (commodity) structure / classification.

Most organisations use United Nations Standard Products and Services Code (UNSPSC) as a basis and build on it according to their organisations' needs. For more information on the various codes, please look at url: https://www.unspsc.org/.

The classification in most organisations is linked to finance natural account codes and this step should be carried out by both purchasing and finance to ensure the category classification is streamlined.

Examples of category classifications include:

UNSPSC Code	UNSPSC Description
44102902	Storage accessories for office machines
44102906	Computer or office equipment cleaning kit
56111500	Workstations and office packages
56111501	Modular reception office packages
44100000	Office machines and their supplies and accessories
44101705	Office machine trays or feeders
53102709	Ambulance officers uniforms
81121505	Economic development consultancy
71161605	Oilfield consultancy services
86132102	Training planning and development consultancy service

Some organisations that I have worked with also create their own category codes. For example:

Category Code	Category Description
S155661	Management Consultancy Services
G267892	Office Consumables

My recommendation is for SME's to work with the procurement team to create category structure for the organisation. Finance should also be involved to map natural accounts to the categories.

In general, it is important to get the master data accurately set up. Organisations should spend efforts analysing vendors that are frequently used and set up contracts against them. The more contracts and catalogues that are set up, the more simplistic the PO requests process becomes.

I understand how difficult the master data elements can be for organisations, if you require additional consulting and would like to discuss approaches to tackle this subject, you contact Revolution Global Services Limited via email Nadeem.Surve1@gmail.com.

- **Catalogue Requests**

This is where a catalogue is set up against a vendor based on a contract with articles and requesters can select items and request a PO for them. A good example of this is a catalogue for Stationery.

Organisations try and implement processes where they try and direct employees towards catalogues or categories to simplify the requisitioning process. I have also observed organisations that do not implement catalogues and, instead, purchasing is heavily involved in the process.

Where catalogues exist, requesters should purchase from them, if no catalogue exists, then follow the non-catalogue process. The advantage of catalogues is that purchasing does not need to get involved during the ordering process. This is because procurement was involved in the process of setting up the initial catalogue with the supplier.

It is important to negotiate as many contracts and catalogues with suppliers to help streamline the purchasing process. If catalogues are unavailable, then the non-catalogue process should be adopted.

- **Non-Catalogue Requests**

This is a request where a catalogue does not exist and the employee would describe the requirement and select the vendors based on requirements.

Organisations have processes where local vendors can be used for items that do not exist in catalogues. Where prices are not fixed, this process is used on a regular basis. Examples of this include management consultancies, agencies and business specific requirements.

Non-Catalogue Requests means, the requester completes a request and enters the item description, price, quantity, supplier and additional information.

Non-Catalogue Requests generally go through some type of procurement approval to review the category that has been selected along with the price and supplier.

- **3 Quotes Process**

This is similar to Non-Catalogue Requests but when no catalogue exists, the process involves the employee obtaining 3 quotes before requesting a PO. The business rule could be conditioned based on category and threshold.

Once the organisation has decided on the processes to adopt, the rest of the process can be defined. For example, if the 3 Quotes Process is adopted, there is a good argument not to implement the procurement approval process because the employee has obtained 3 quotes from suppliers and selected the best one. It means procurement can retrospectively run reports to audit spend against specialist categories and thresholds to ensure that the correct process is being followed by the business users.

Other examples that I have implemented include ensuring the buyer is always part of the approval process to ensure that the employee has raised the request correctly against the best possible supplier. Global organisations tend to have a mix of both and have specific commodities that require additional approval (specialist category).

Process Step: Financial Approval

Financial Approval

- Cost Center / Budget Approval
- Delegation of Authority

This step involves the approval of requisitions (request for PO). Some organisations implement processes where line managers approve all purchase requests and this means no additional approval is required. The benefit of this is that purchase requests go through a single approval step and PO's are generated efficiently. This approach generally works well for small businesses where the number of employees is very low.

I have been involved with process workshops where large organisations require more complex approval processes based on controls and compliance. For example, the first approval step is sent to the line manager, followed by financial approval based on the budget code and then follows the approval hierarchy until the person with the right authorisation level approves the purchase request.

The problem such complicated workflows brings to organisations is the delay in PO's reaching suppliers on time. It is important to find the right balance when implementing processes related to approvals. I have been involved in process design workshops where the business initially required 18 approval steps but eventually settled to 8, based on approval limits.

Process Step: Purchasing Approval

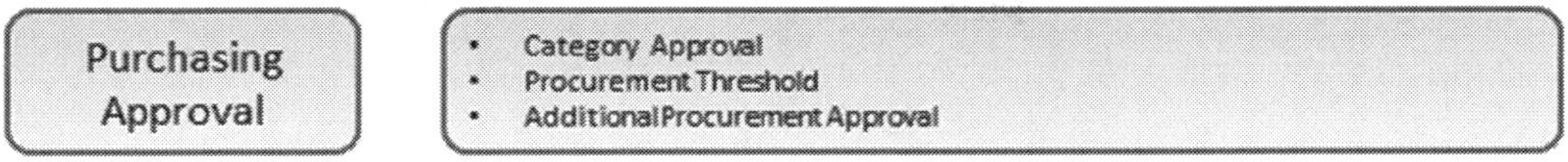

Purchasing Approval	• Category Approval • Procurement Threshold • Additional Procurement Approval

This step is depends on the purchasing team agreeing with the details on the purchase request. Some organisations implement the below processes:

- **Category Approval**

This is where specialist categories are sent for approval for operational buyers to complete. They review the contents and ensure the vendor selected and price information entered by the requester is correct. At this stage, they can amend, reject or approve the purchase request.

- **Procurement Threshold Approval**

Some organisations look at threshold as a way to check requests against the strategic procurement policies. It is important that the procurement approvals benefit the corporate strategy. I have worked with some organisations where they have implemented a 3 step process based on threshold and category. For example, the first procurement step is sent to the operational buyer, the second procurement step is sent to the strategic procurement buyer and the final step based on threshold is sent to the head of procurement. The threshold ranged from 50,000 to 500,000,000.

- **Non-Catalogue Request Approval**

Most organisations that I have worked with implement processes around non-catalogue requests where the operational buyer is involved in the processing of the purchase request. Some organisations create requests but do not enter a supplier at the point of ordering. In this case, the operational buyer would find the best supplier and edit the request and approve the purchase request.

In summary, there are various ways to implement processes around procurement approval. Some organisations do not implement processes for procurement as there is no requirement for this function. Others tend to have procurement approval based on commodity, type of request or threshold. It is important to understand what the organisation purchases and how it is purchased to decide what should and should not go through this approval process. As an example, some procurement functions may want to see non-catalogue purchase requests related to mobile phone purchases but not interested to see management consultancy purchases. In this case, mobile phone purchases would go for non-catalogue approval.

Process Step: Purchase Order Creation (PO)

PO Creation

- ManualPO Creation
- Automated PO Creation
- PO Amendment

Once all approvals are completed, the next process step relates to the physical creation of the PO before it is sent to the supplier. From my experience of implementing processes and system, I have listed 3 main ways PO's can be created:

- **Interface PO from third party systems**

Some large organisations have various ways for PO's to be created. One of the ways is from third party or legacy systems to send an interface to create a PO in your procurement system. This means sales orders are created in another system and, once approved, they are transferred into your system. A good example of this is where businesses raise sales order for goods that are sold in a filling station. The filling station places the order via an online ordering system and the order is then interfaced to your procurement system in order for you to fulfil this order.

- **Operational Buyers Pool**

Some organisations adopt a manual process to generate PO's. This can be for non-catalogue requests, where the requester has created a purchase request. The operational buyer would review the shopping cart and check whether the price and supplier is consistent with the procurement strategy. The operational buyer would also check if any surplus stock is available within the business before generating the PO.

Organisations tend to have designated operational buyers based on commodity. For example, anything related to corporate services would be handled by a set of buyers and anything related to Business Travel would be managed by another set of buyers.

See illustration below:

Buyer Responsibility	**Commodity Description**
Buyer A	Management Consultancy Services
Buyer B	Office Consumables
Buyer C	IT Hardware
Buyer D	IT Software

From my experience, some global businesses also like to review specific catalogue based purchase requests in the buyers' pool. This is for items of high value and low volume. Examples include printers or drinks vending machines. The operational buyer may want to review the requests before creating a PO.

- **Automatic Creation of PO based on type of purchase request**

Depending on the procurement strategy for the organisation and the procurement system implemented, PO's can also be automatically created once the purchase request has been fully approved. The types of PO's that normally get automatically generated include:

- Contract related PO's
- Catalogue based PO's
- Specific PO's based on customised conditions (exception listed)

The general rule is, if procurement has been involved in the setup of the master data (contract / catalogue) before a purchase request is created, then they are less likely to want to manually create the PO.

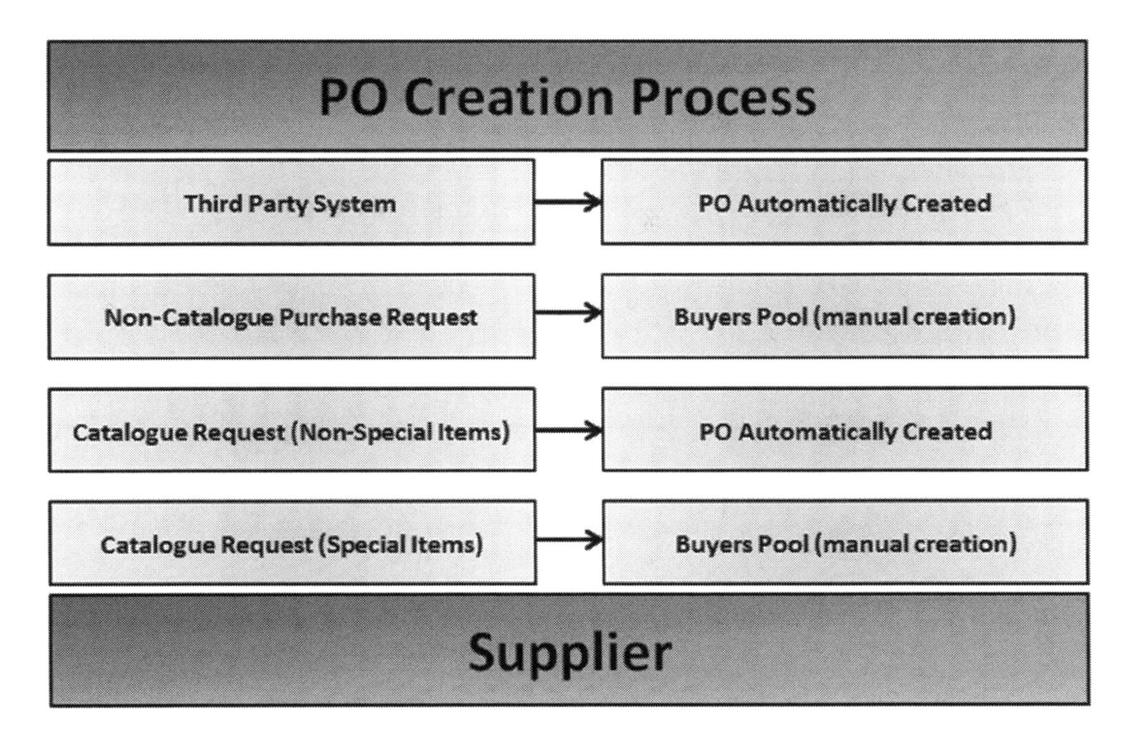

From experience, most businesses try and utilise contracts / catalogues and vendor lists to direct requesters towards requesting from preferred suppliers. This is not always achievable and depends on the maturity of the purchasing department. Many organisations I have worked with have started to implement initiatives where PO's must be raised in order for suppliers to be paid (no PO, no Pay). This means that where in the past requesters were able to pay invoices without the need for a PO, they now have to create purchase requests. This is a change to the process and should be implemented in phases without impacting the business.

Process Step: Purchase Order sent to Supplier

PO Sent to Supplier

- PO Output: Email, Fax, XML, Print

The next process step in the Purchase to Receipt cycle is the PO output to the supplier. There has been a big shift to automate the sending of the PO's to suppliers. Most organisations use procurement systems (software) to send PO's to suppliers. The main types of PO Outputs include:

- E-Mail
- XML
- Fax
- Print
- Marketplace
- Supplier Portal

Nowadays most suppliers have email addresses and will accept a PDF PO sent to their email address. Some organisations have contracts in place where they expect the PO to be sent into their ordering systems via XML or EDI technology.

Some larger organisations implement supplier portals for suppliers to retrieve PO's. I have also found organisations that are a part of a marketplace, where suppliers can retrieve PO's from organisations.

Some suppliers also send order acknowledgments to confirm when delivery will be made. This helps the requester understand when the PO will be delivered and for goods receipts to be made.

In summary, the PO output medium can vary depending on size of the business and supplier. Most suppliers are happy to accept for PO's to be sent via email, whilst other suppliers may want you to send the PO directly into their supply chain management systems.

Process Step: Purchase Order – Goods Receipts

The final process step in the Purchase to Receipt cycle is the goods receipting (confirmations) against the PO based on the business rules. This step is in confirming that everything ordered on the PO was delivered and the business is happy for invoice to be paid.

This step sometimes becomes an overhead and businesses tend to adopt auto-receipting for high volume but low value items such as stationery. Others send out reminder notifications to requesters based on delivery dates to confirm the PO. This only works if the requester has populated the right delivery dates.

The various types of processes that I have been involved in include:

- Goods Receipt Reminders based on Delivery Date
- Automatic Goods Receipting Rules
- Invoice Tolerances to allow over delivery of PO Items
- The ability to goods receipt via email without the need to log into a procurement system

The goods receipting process is of great importance for the invoice processing process within the Source to Pay (S2P) process where the business adopts a 3 way match scenario and invoices need to match the goods receipts.

Goods receipting can be completed if the PO is not raised correctly or amended accordingly depending on the invoice. Organisations need to understand the requesters are not finance clerks and do not understand the financial implications of incorrect receipting. Supplier payments can be delayed and legal action taken if they do not get paid on time. Also, incorrect accounting can be reported if receipting is not done accurately.

3. Invoice Processing

The final process area within the procurement roadmap is Invoice Processing and Payment. This is an important step for all vendors and businesses. If the processes are not efficiently managed, vendors may not receive payment on time, which could lead to legal action or dissatisfaction from the vendor.

Invoice processing involves the handling of incoming invoices from arrival to post. Invoices have many variations and types. In general, invoices are grouped into two types:

1. Invoices associated with a request or purchase order
2. Invoices that do not have an associated request (no purchase order) (from Wikepedia).

Most organizations have clear instructions regarding the processing of incoming invoices. Different sets of instructions are commonly found in most organizations regarding the handling of purchase order invoices or non-purchase order invoices. The main department that processes invoices is known as accounts payable department. The process involving a supplier invoice is also known as purchase-to-pay (from Wikepedia).

The key areas that will be discussed include:

- PO / Non-PO Invoice
- Invoice Matching Rules / Invoice Discrepancies
- Invoicing Coding Rules
- Supplier Invoice Payment

Invoice processing is a complex subject as it has many implications. With organisations implementing electronic tools to automate the matching process, this process should be 'touchless', but from my experience of implementing processes, it is by far a 'touchless' process.

There are many reasons why it sometimes does not work as effectively as it was designed. Some of the blame is on the supplier sending invoices incorrectly with the wrong information, sometimes it is due to the requester not receipting the PO on time and sometimes it is a mixture of the two and also technology not capturing the invoice details correctly.

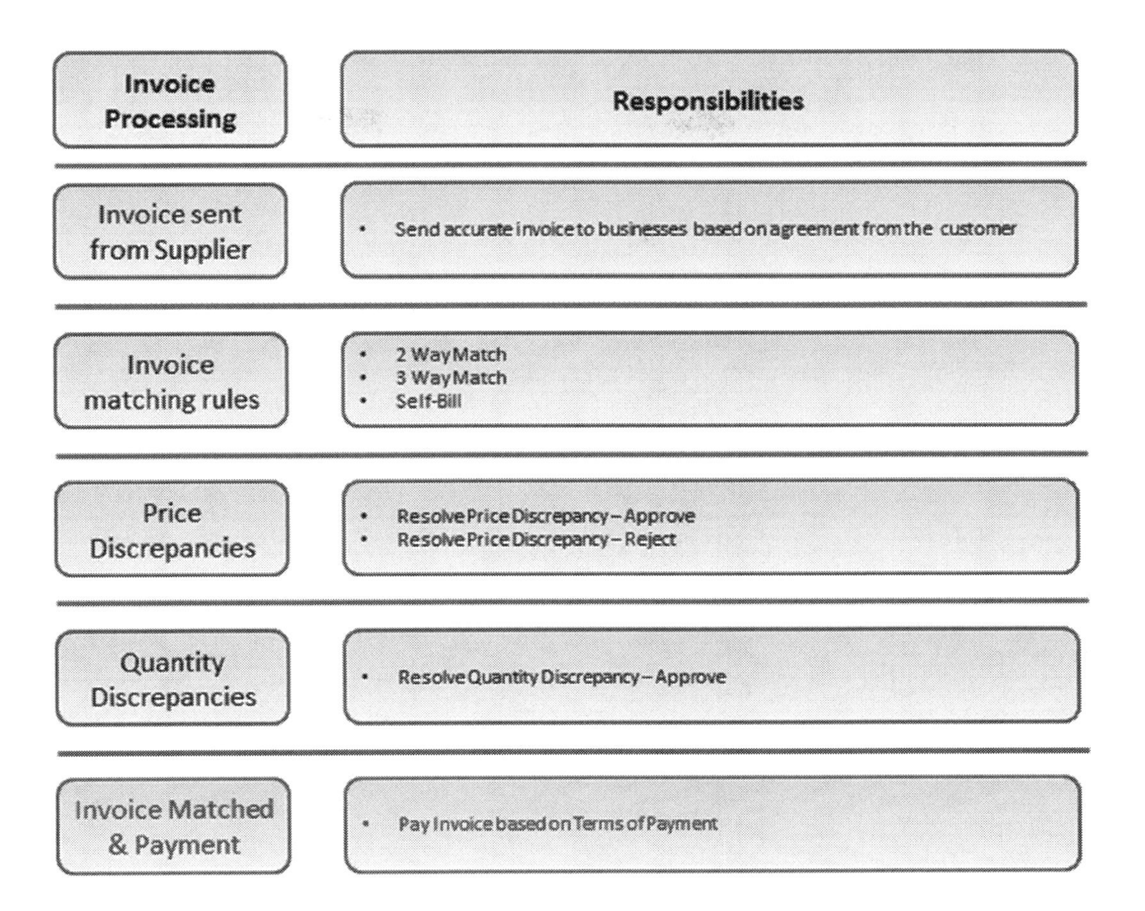

The above table illustrates the main **responsibilities** within the Invoice Processing process steps.

- **Invoice Processing (2 / 3 Way Match, Self-Billing)**

  The Accounts Payable (AP) Team will process invoices based on the invoice sent by suppliers. There are various ways for invoices to be matched. The 3 most common ways include:

- **2 Way Match:** The accounts payable department receives the purchase order and invoice documents and the two will be checked to ensure consistency against the PO.

- **3 Way Match:** The accounts payable department receives the purchase order, invoice, and confirmation documents and the three will be checked to ensure consistency against the PO.

- **Self-Bill:** Once a goods receipt has been posted, the procurement system will automatically generate an invoice based on the confirmation and payment processes will make payment to the supplier.

The process below shows the difference between a 2 and 3 way match:

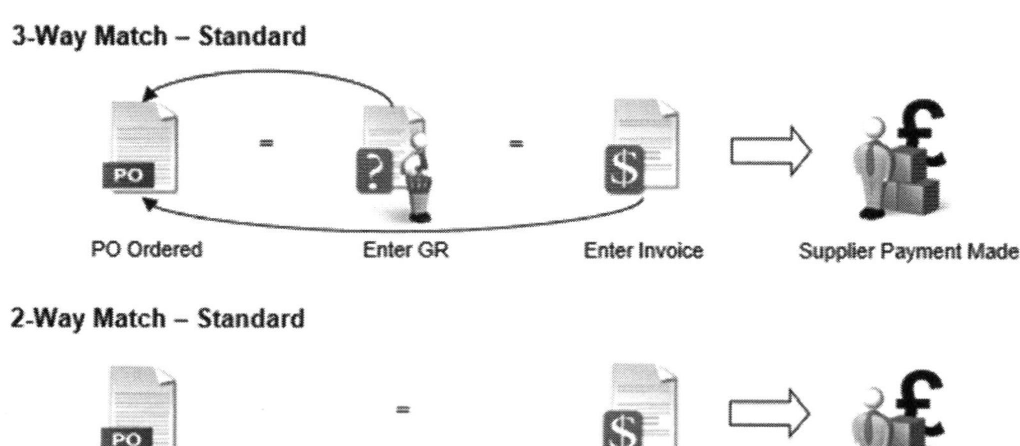

- ## Payment to Supplier

This process step is where the organisation makes payment to the vendor and will be discussed in the Invoice Processing process step.

Let's now discuss this topic in more detail.

Process Step: Invoice sent from Supplier

Invoice sent from Supplier	• Send accurate invoice to businesses based on agreement from the customer

The process starts with the supplier sending an invoice to the organisation. There are some key points that should be highlighted below:

- The supplier should send a PO related invoice based on the goods / services delivered
- The supplier should send a non-PO related invoice based on agreement and delivery of goods / services
- The supplier invoice should reflect the goods / services delivered
- The supplier invoice should be accurate and consistent
- Suppliers should not send invoices before the goods / services have been delivered
- If suppliers choose to partially deliver goods / services, then this should be consistent

Some organisations have terms and conditions that the supplier should agree to, in order for invoices to be processed correctly.

In summary, the above key points are simple to understand, but from my observations, suppliers have automated processes on their side and sometimes do not adhere to the agreement between them and the business. If suppliers do not adopt the key points there may be delays in processing the invoice by the customer. There may be a lot of rejected invoices or invoices in status query. Suppliers have to contact the customer for payment.

Process Step: Invoice matching rules

Invoice matching rules

- 2 Way Match
- 3 Way Match
- Self-Bill

Organisations adopt invoice-matching rules that safeguard the business and give the right balance to allow suppliers to get paid on time. The matching rules include the below:

- **2 Way Match**

The accounts payable department receives the purchase order and invoice documents and the two will be checked to ensure consistency against the PO.

Due to business and legislative policies, this process is not adopted for all types of spend by organisations because suppliers could get paid for high value purchases before goods / services have been delivered. This process works more effectively for high volume, low value products such as stationery. 2-way match can help organisations' achieve a high rate of auto match.

- **3 Way Match**

The accounts payable department receives the purchase order, invoice, and confirmation documents and the three will be checked to ensure consistency against the PO.

I have worked with businesses that adopt only 3-way match for all PO related purchases, which means a goods receipt must exist. This means there is reliance on requesters confirming PO's before invoices are sent from the supplier. I have noticed that when this process is adopted, it does cause a delay in invoices getting posted in time for payment. Requesters do not always goods receipts on time, leading to suppliers querying for payment. Reminder notifications can sometimes help increase invoice processing.

- **Self-Bill**

Once a goods receipt has been posted, the procurement system will automatically generate an invoice based on the confirmation and payment processes will make payment to the supplier.

I have observed companies use this function when the PO always matches the invoice. Instead of suppliers sending invoices, the business may automatically receipt the PO, which then creates an invoice. There are specific types of requests where self-billing works brilliantly.

Along with the above matching rules, organisations also have processes related to non-PO invoices (Finance Invoices). This is where the business has specified a number of suppliers where a PO is not required because of the importance of receiving the goods and processing of payments. The PO process works for 90% of the types of purchasing but there is always 10% depending on type of business where suppliers would invoice without a PO.

The diagram below demonstrates the exception handling during the invoice processing phase. Some companies agree on tolerances where an invoice can be posted 5% above the PO value.

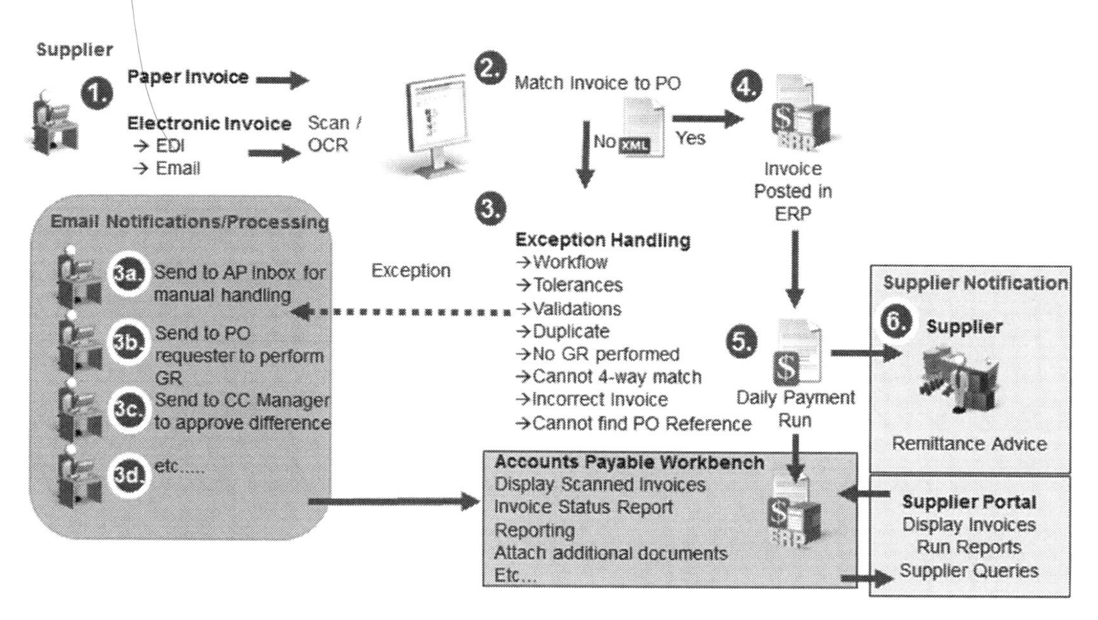

Other exception handling processes include identification of duplicate invoices sent by the supplier and incorrect PO reference.

Process Step: Price Discrepancies

Price Discrepancies

- Resolve Price Discrepancy – Approve
- Resolve Price Discrepancy – Reject

The Accounts Payable (AP) Team receives invoices from vendors for Purchase Order related goods and services. Invoices will be matched and paid when there is a three-way match (the information on the PO, the goods receipt (confirmation) and the invoice must all agree.

Invoices may be blocked for payment when there is a discrepancy in the match between the price of the purchase order, goods confirmation, and the invoice. When an invoice is blocked, various processes are implemented by businesses to resolve them.

If a blocked invoice isn't resolved, the vendor will not be paid, commitments may not incur properly against the budget (you may think you have more money to spend than you actually do), which is incorrect.

Organisations adopt various processes to resolve price queries. Some of the processes I have implemented are explained below:

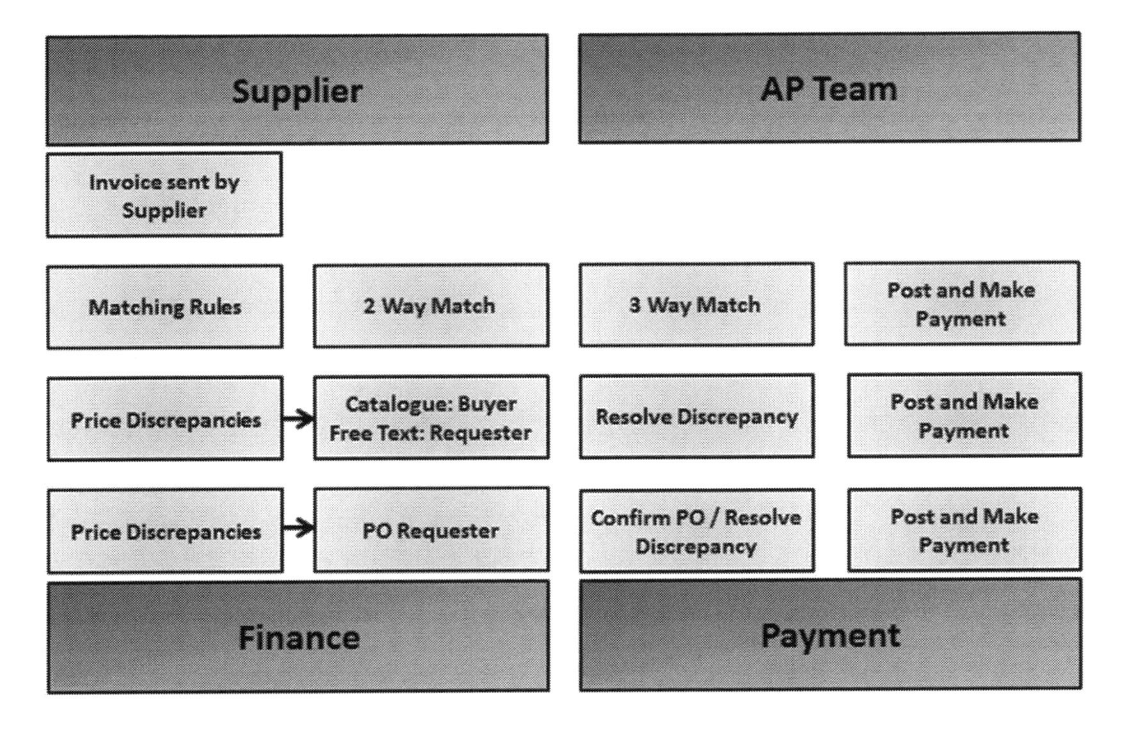

Organisations that I have previously helped to implement procurement in the past have managed price discrepancies in different ways. Some organisations have expected finance departments to resolve price discrepancies and contact the supplier directly. Some organisations differentiate between the types of PO's and route it accordingly.

Example 1:

Type of Purchase	Resolve Group
Catalogue PO	Operational Buyer
Non-Catalogue PO	Requester
Contracted PO	Contract Person Responsible

Example 2:

Type of Purchase	Resolve Group
Catalogue PO	Operational Buyer
Non-Catalogue PO	Operational Buyer
Contracted PO	Contract Person Responsible

Example 3:

Type of Purchase	Resolve Group
Catalogue PO	Requester
Non-Catalogue PO	Requester
Contracted PO	Requester

Once the price discrepancy has been resolved, the invoice will match the PO and the payment process will start. Sometimes organisations adopt price tolerances to allow invoices to match PO's (5%).

Process Step: Quantity Discrepancies

Quantity Discrepancies

- Resolve Quantity Discrepancy – Approve

Invoices are blocked for payment when there is a discrepancy in the 3-way match between the quantities on the Purchase Order, Goods Receipt(s) (Confirmation), and the Invoice(s).

When an invoice related to a PO is entered, the process is for the AP Team to attempt to match the invoice quantity to the net received quantity as shown on the PO at the time the invoice is processed. In other words, the quantity already received on the system that is yet to be matched to an invoice. A quantity mismatch may occur when the invoice quantity is greater than the available received quantity on the current PO.

For example:

Quantity Discrepancy	Explanation
PO Quantity: 10 Writing Pads Goods Receipt: 0 (GRN Missing Invoice Quantity: 10 Writing Pads	To resolve this, the requester needs to confirm the goods on the PO.
PO Quantity: 2 Mobile Phones Goods Receipt Quantity: 2 Mobile Phones Invoice Quantity: 20 Mobile Phones	The invoice has been sent for more than the PO. The requester can either accept the invoice, in which case, amending the PO and then confirming it, or reject the invoice and ask the supplier to send a revised version.
PO Quantity: 10 Laptops Goods Receipt Quantity: 10 Laptops Invoice #1 Quantity:10 Laptops Invoice #2 Quantity: 10 Laptops	The supplier has sent the same invoice twice. Reject the invoice and contact the supplier as the invoice might be a duplicate.

Some organisations set up invoice quantity tolerances to allow quantity values to match against the PO. Others do not allow this flexibility and if the quantity does not match to the confirmation, an email is sent to the requester asking them to confirm the PO or request to amend the PO accordingly. Once confirmed, the Invoice will match the PO.

Process Step: Invoice Matched & Payment

Invoice Matched & Payment	• Pay Invoice based on Terms of Payment

This is the final process step within the Invoice Processing roadmap and covers the physical payment of the invoice based on the payment terms set up against the supplier.

At this point, I would like to mention that apart from PO related invoices, there could be Non-PO related invoices where a PO is not required based on business exceptions. For Non-PO related invoices, the AP Team would either manually code and send for approval or route the invoice to the relevant department to code and send for approval.

Once approval is complete, then the invoice will also be ready for payment. The approvals for Non-PO related invoices can vary. It could be a single financial step approval or depending on approval limits, it could go based on the financial hierarchy.

In summary, the importance of an efficient invoice process cannot be understated; the quicker the organisation can progress invoices to customers and clients, the faster the business can process and make payment and, thereby, have a massive positive impact on cash flow. Alternatively, delays to payment can quickly have a knock-on impact on your corporate image with incorrect financial figures in your accounts.

Organisations implement intelligent software to help streamline and process invoices efficiently. The mix of people, process and technology can help the processing and payments of invoices work more effectively.

STEP 3

PROJECT STRATEGIES

STEP 3 – Project Strategies

Summary of Step 3:

There are a number of processes that take place within the project strategies process area. Before a project is started, a PID needs is created which involves a business case and various evaluations completed. What problem are you trying to resolve? What type of return on investment (ROI) do you expect? What does the project delivery look like in terms of resource, communication and timeframes?

These are typical questions that need answering and, also, does the project strategy complement the corporate goals of the organisation? There are examples of various resourcing models for small and large projects.

The project management methodology has an impact on the outcome of a procurement system. I tend to use a hybrid of Waterfall / Agile and many organisations where I have implemented software seem to adopt the same.

The world of procurement is not as simple as we would like it to be and the previous two steps have demonstrated this. The procurement strategy and procurement roadmap must be consistent and should play a big part on the project strategy that is implemented to get procurement processes working within the organisation.

From my knowledge, the following steps are crucial when implementing a successful procurement system:

- Project initiation processes
- Resources
- Project Phases
- Testing and Communication
- Implementation Processes
- High Level Design Strategies
- Strategic Frameworks

The diagram below illustrates the areas involved within the Project Strategy:

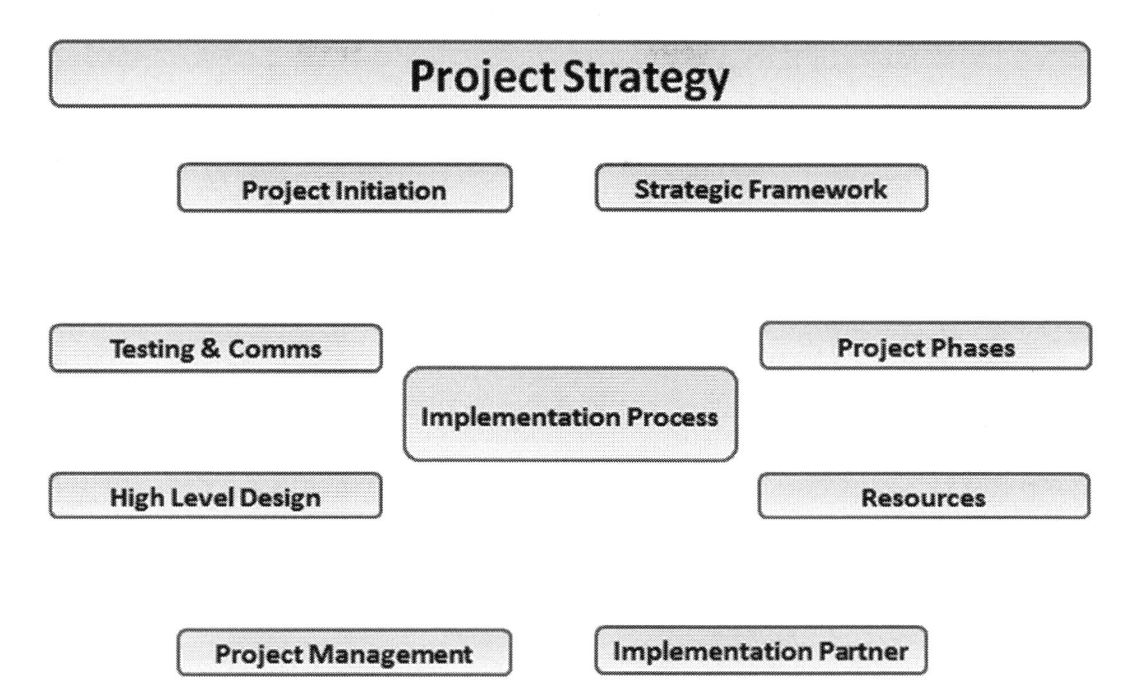

Process Step: Project Initiation Processes

Project Initiation	• Business Case • Process Initiation Document • Presentation to Stakeholders • Approval from Stakeholders

The initiation process is to start a project. One of the key parts of the initiation process that always raises questions is the business case. This is the document that is produced to demonstrate the finances and the cost-benefit the organisation would need to undertake for the project to progress forward. Therefore, I would recommend creating this as part of the requirement before the project is fully initialised.

In the real world, what tends to happen is that people who are responsible in their own areas identify possible solutions to a business need. Based on this, a business case is created with solutions. From experience, once enough people are engaged in the process a project is created.

The project initiation phase takes into consideration the business case and identifies the project objectives and how they will be achieved. The types of questions that make up this phase include:

- What is the role of the project?
- How is the project going to deliver the requirements / business case?
- Does the business case require a project?
- Who is the customer?
- Where will the budget come from?
- Who is going to implement the project?
- Who is going to do the work?

The answers to these questions may seem obvious but there is usually still some room for uncertainty. This phase is to gather the answers to questions so that everyone understands the deliverables. All projects need a business case before they can be properly initialised. The business case is written by various people within the organisation and should demonstrate at least the following basic points:

- How the problem will be resolved with the initiation of the project
- The main reasons for initiating the project
- What potential resources are required
- The creation of an action plan (project plan)
- Identify the benefits and challenges
- What specific next step is needed to get the project started
- Additional requirements, legal, control, compliance, reporting

The business case is part of the Project Initiation Process and should be completed based on an understanding of what is possible within the organisation. Other documents that should be created as part of the project kick off include the Project Initiation Document (PID), a detailed document that has the following:

- Project Scope
- Project Statement
- Project Background
- Financial Aspects
- Any assumptions, dependencies, constraints
- Various Plans
- Identify top project risks
- Project Responsibilities

The above is a summary of the main areas that should be considered in the PID. The greater the detail, the more effective the PID becomes as it helps the stakeholders to understand what problems the project is trying to resolve. There are lots of project methodologies in the market that can help with writing a successful PID.

The PID is written to obtain approval from stakeholders and people that are close to the project area. To demonstrate the effectiveness of a PID, I would recommend using PowerPoint slides to highlight the main points and present this to the senior management. It is also recommended to have flow diagrams, graphical images and roadmaps to assist with the decision making process.

Financial aspects of the project should be analysed and documented. Any budgetary constraints should be identified and assumptions used to estimate project delivery.

The PID should estimate the resources required to deliver the project. Also, how the resources will be utilised against each phase of the project delivery phases.

Now that we understand the importance of the project initiation process, let's bring it into the subject of procurement. Typically, procurement is closely integrated with financial systems and, as a result, most projects related to procurement start off with financial intentions. In other words, procurement and finance come together as a package and would generally be delivered together.

When creating the PID and Business Case, it is important to focus on the right areas of procurement and not just focus on finance or procurement. Businesses should look at the bigger picture and the integration between procurement and finance.

In summary, the Project Initiation Processes is one of most important phases and is the main contributor for getting a project approved. The PID / business case should be detailed and written in a language which the stakeholders can understand. Visual aids should be used to highlight the costs / benefits, risks and opportunities. The financial aspect of the project initiation process should be explained with any assumptions. The success of a project depends on the project initiation and agreement from the stakeholders.

Let's now take a deeper look into the various sections that is part of the Project Strategies for procurement.

Project Step: Resources

Resources	• Project Manager • Consultants / Architect • Business Analysts	• Subject Matter Experts • Testers • Developers

Whilst implementing finance and procurement projects, I have observed various resourcing models. The resourcing depends on the scope of the project. For example, is the project a procurement led change to people, process and technology or is it a transformation programme where finance is also part of the project.

I have worked on standalone procurement projects where only procurement was impacted and I have also worked on large transformation programmes where finance, procurement and cash management has been part of the scope. This section will discuss the different resource models required from a procurement perspective.

It is important to note that the business case will have some details about resources and the types of resources required to make this work. From my experience, resourcing is always difficult to estimate until the project has kicked off and, by understanding the requirements, organisations can start building a picture of the types of resources that are required. Some business resources are required to make this happen and include subject matter experts (SME's) and Business Analysts (BA's). These types of resource help identify the requirements and document them.

Sometimes resourcing proposals from implementation partners are adopted and resourcing is budgeted based on the proposals.

Resourcing: Standalone Procurement Project

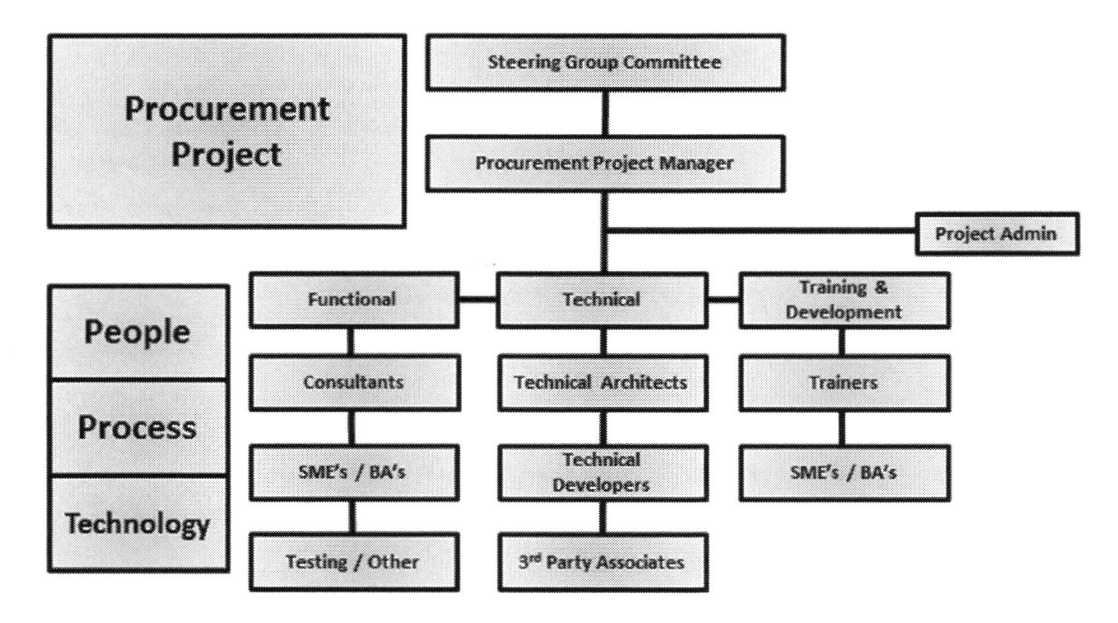

The above diagram illustrates the types of resources required for a standalone procurement implementation for people, processes and technology.

Resourcing: Finance & Procurement Projects

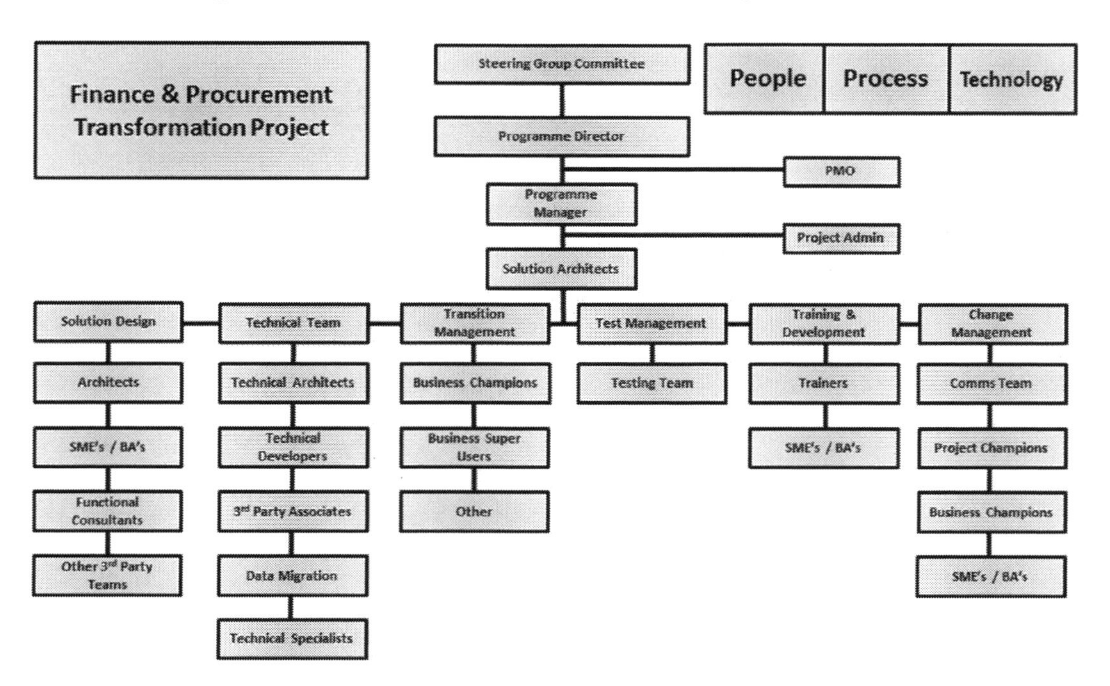

The above diagram illustrates the types of resources required for a finance & procurement implementation for people, processes and technology.

From the two resourcing diagrams, it is clear to see that the size of project determines the types of resources required. I have also implemented smaller procurement functions where the system integrator (IS) managed the project including resources and I was representing the organisation with multiple responsibilities.

Standalone (Procurement) Small Projects:

- 1 x Project Manager
- 1 x Functional / 1 x Technical Consultants
- Business Team: 1 or 2 x SME to cover all responsibilities including:
  - Business Analyst
  - Business Functional Areas
  - Technical Functional Areas
  - Consultant
  - Training & Development
  - Change Management
  - Testing

I was involved in and implemented a project where an outdated catalogue management system was upgraded with a new cloud based catalogue management system. The scope was to change systems and also to change the processes linked to the management of the catalogues. With technology related projects, there is always an element of change to processes and sometimes automation can lead to changes to people as well.

The above resources demonstrate a very aggressive project team. As the project scope was very small and the timeline was 6 months to deliver, 4 to 5 resources working on the project was sufficient. The key resource from a business perspective was the Subject Matter Expert (SME). This resource had multiple roles within the project and understood the scope and understanding of what problems the implementation was going to resolve.

The smaller projects tend to run between 3 to 9 months and target specific business departments and roles. In my example of implementing a new catalogue management system, the people impacted were requesters (raising catalogue purchase requests), buyers (uploading catalogue content) and the various sites (connectivity / firewall).

Standalone (Procurement) Medium Projects:

- 1 x Project Manager
- 1 x Project Admin
- 2 x Functional / 2 x Technical Consultants (Architects)
- 2 x Business SME's
- 1 x Business Analyst
- 1 x Training & Development
- 1 x Change Management
- 2 x Testing
- 1 x 3rd Party Association

When comparing the above types of resources against the small project, it is clear to see that the resource model has three times more resources versus the small project. This is due to the fact that a medium procurement project has extended scope based on business requirements. A good example of this is where a procurement system is to be upgraded from an older version to a newer version and, at the same time, the business look to increase the functions within it. In other words, add new functionality and introduce new processes.

The sort of timelines for upgrade projects could be between 6 to 12 months with various cycles of regression testing at different points of the software lifecycle.

Large Finance & Procurement Projects (Programme):

- 1 x Programme Director
- 1 x Project Manager
- 3 x Project Management Officers (PMO)
- 2 x Project Admin
- 3 x Solution Architects (1 per stream (Finance, Procurement, Reporting)
- 1 x Solution Design Lead
- 3 x Business Architects (1 per stream (Finance, Procurement, Reporting)
- 6 x Functional Consultants
- 5 x Technical Consultants (Developers)
- 6 x Business SME's
- 2 x Business Analyst
- 1 x Training & Development Lead
- 4 x Trainers
- 4 x Change Management
- 1 x Testing Lead
- 1 x Change Management Lead
- 4 x Testing
- 3 x 3rd Party Association
- 6 x Super Users (part time)
- 10 x Others

From the above resource types, there are a significant number of resources required for large scale implementations that include finance, procurement, reporting and other areas.

It is important to define the key business resource as early as possible as experience has shown me that this can be a challenge. Releasing key business representatives for the length of a project can be difficult as large transformation programmes can last between 3 to 5 years.

In summary, the resource allocation on projects can vary depending on the scope, size and integration partner. Small projects may have 4/5 resources allocated and large programmes may have 50 plus resources to deliver the project.

Now that we understand the main resources required on procurement projects, let's focus on how the resources can be applied to the project phases.

Project Step: Project Phases

Project Phases	• Solution Design • Build • Test	• UAT • Data Migration • Production Cutover

The project phases are very much dependent on the type of project methodology adopted by the project team. This topic will be discussed in Step 4 in more detail. In this step, I look to cover the main phases that organisations generally adopt when implementing a procurement system and describe the roles and responsibilities for each.

When comparing the 3 different types of projects (small, medium and large), the roles and responsibilities within each project phase are similar but, as the project size and scope increases, so does the complexity and responsibilities.

I have found the BA's, Functional Consultants, SME's are involved throughout the different project phases. Continuity is very important on a project or programme. I have worked on projects where project resources have been released causing knowledge gaps, leading to disruption and, consequently, impacting on the project deliverables.

- The BA mainly gathers and documents requirements
- The functional consultant will map the requirements to the functionality available and identify where enhancements are required.
- SME's are involved to map processes and help with gathering requirements.

The diagram below illustrates the project phases and the **roles** and **responsibilities** within each main phase:

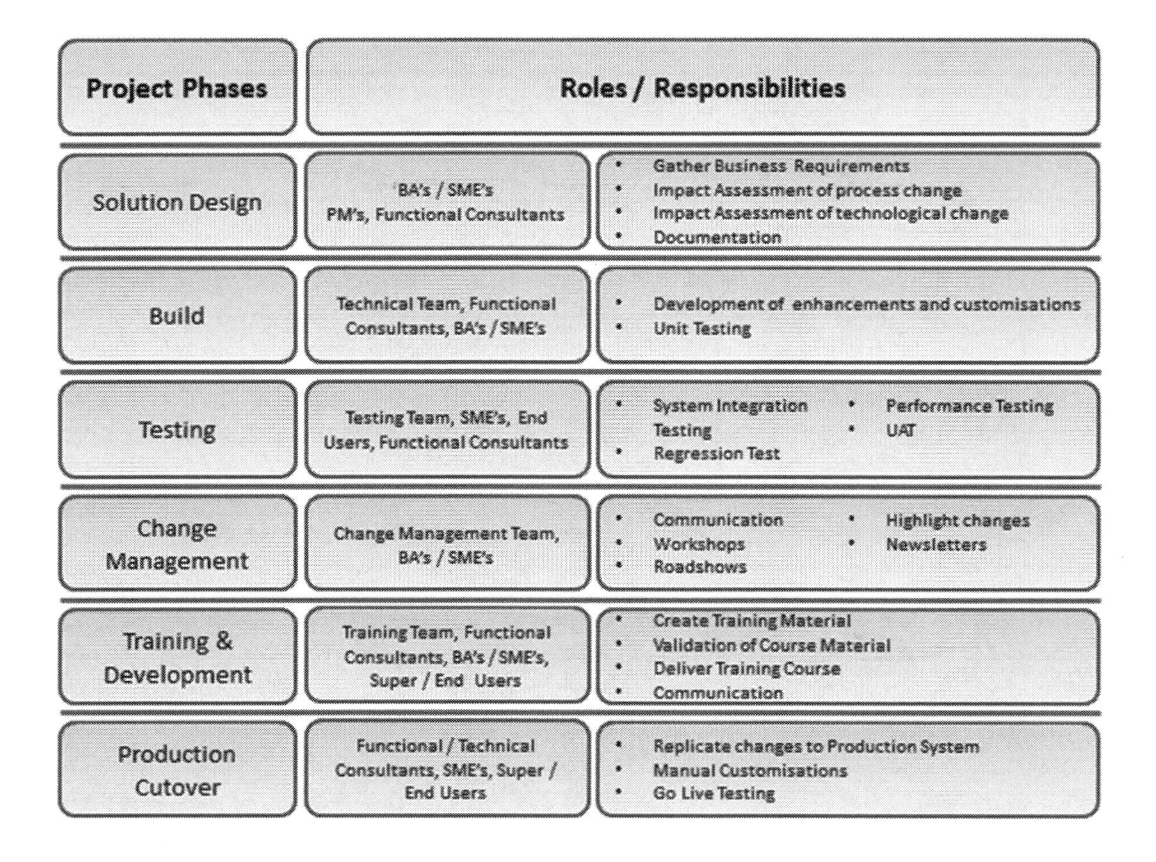

As mentioned earlier, the SME's will assist the BA to clarify the requirements and check with the business community. The 3 parties (BA, SME and Functional Consultant) will validate the requirements and produce a requirements register and a gap list that requires further investigation.

Projects are not always easy to deliver and there are many challenges faced as you undergo the project phases. Dynamics such as new requirements or an altering scope of project deliverables due to business timelines should be factored into the project phases. Even if a project phase has been completed, there has to be processes in place to accommodate new requirements and adjustments to existing requirements (change requests).

Project Step: Testing and Communication

Testing and Communication	• Various phases of testing • Various stages for communication

It is important to engage with the appropriate business representatives for both communication and testing phases because you want to provide the appropriate information at the right time. Communication comes under Change Management and it will be discussed in more detail as part of Step 5.

Communication

Most organisations adopt communication strategies by demonstrating roadmaps to stakeholders, to keep them informed of the statuses, as well as process design workshops / walkthroughs, to keep the wider business updated on the processes and solutions.

There is a fine line between too much information versus not enough. The balance is not easy and the environment, culture and geographic location can all have an impact on communication. Some organisations adopt daily stand ups whilst others have weekly stand up meetings. I have worked with organisations that have daily 9am stand up meetings which last between 15 to 30 minutes within the teams and weekly stand ups which last up to an hour.

I am not convinced that daily stand ups are as effective as weekly stand ups. I prefer weekly meetings and, where required, focused sessions to resolve project issues. This approach has proved more beneficial and productive on all projects that I have worked on.

Nowadays, communication is a lot easier thanks to collaboration tools. You can now share screens as well as conference and telepresence to anyone anywhere. For large projects, which are across multiple regions, communication is key and collaboration tools can facilitate this.

Another key aspect of communication is being able to interconnect within the project team. I have worked on projects where each team communicates well within their own work stream but does not communicate to other teams as effectively. Procurement is an area that feeds into Finance / Purchasing and communication needs to be integrated between the two areas. From experience, if this is not managed, you often find issues during the user acceptance testing and this sometimes causes problems/challenges on the project.

Communication should be made to all levels at the right time. Defining the right time can sometime be tricky and could have negative impacts on the project. Having too many scheduled meetings can also become onerous and counterproductive.

The following has worked well for me when implementing small projects:

- Weekly Stream Meetings
- Monthly Project Stand Up Meetings
- Ad-hoc Focused Meetings
- Weekly Integration Meetings with all streams

Testing

The testing strategy should be defined as part of the project strategies. Most organisations decide on their testing strategy when they have adopted a project methodology.

A typical procurement project will have various testing phases including:

- **Unit Testing**

  Testing enhancements and customisations in small chunks and completed by the technical team

- **Functional Testing**

  Functional Testing is based on customisations and enhancements, not based on business requirements, and completed by functional consultants

- **System Integration Testing**

  Testing customised and enhancements against business requirements, including negative testing completed by the testing team and various BA's

- **User Acceptance Testing**

  User acceptance testing (UAT) is the last phase of the software testing process. During UAT, actual end users test the software to make sure it can handle required tasks in real-world scenarios and according to specifications. This is normally end to end testing with integration with other areas such as finance and reporting.

- **Performance Testing**

  Performance Testing is testing the quality of the system including reliability, responsiveness, stability and technical resources.

- **Regression Testing**

  Regression testing is testing which verifies that software, which was previously developed and tested, still performs correctly after it was changed. Changes may include software enhancements, patches, configuration changes, etc.

In summary, the communication and testing phases are very important to the success of project strategies. The strategies should be defined as part of the project kick off process.

I have found it beneficial to test processes as early as possible in the functional testing phase. This way, I have managed to resolve any defects early in the project phases rather than identifying them in later testing phases.

For me, the key is the functional consultant completing the testing with a good understanding of the requirements. Attention to detail during the testing phase is also vital and the success of testing can sometime be measured during UAT when the testing should run smoothly with less identified problems.

Another key attribute to the success of a procurement system is the scope of the testing completing by the team. I try to test as much positive and negative testing as I can to give myself the assurance that the procurement system works and is fit for purpose.

Project Step: Implementation Processes

Implementation Processes	• Waterfall Vs. Agile

There are many implementation processes available in the market when implementing procurement systems. It is important to decide on the implement process during the early stages of the project.

Implementation is the process that turns strategies and plans into actions in order to accomplish strategic objectives. Implementing your strategic plan is as important, or even more important, than your strategy.

A strategic plan provides the organisation with the roadmap it needs to deliver a specific strategic direction and set of performance goals, be successful and deliver customer value. However, a strategic plan does not always guarantee that the requirements are fulfilled compared to having a roadmap which guarantees the requirements are met.

These are the main areas within the implementation process.

Implementation Process (Strategic Plan)

Defined Ownership

Defined Communication

Defined Accountability

Meaningful Plan

Status Reporting

Experience has shown me that accountability and ownership on procurement projects is very important. A strategic plan should incorporate these factors with clear reporting structures to confirm the status of the tasks.

Communication strategies should be embedded into the implementation process to channel important information to the project team. The bigger the project, the more appropriate channels of communication should be deployed. Some projects I have worked with have had large sheets of project plans, status reports on walls for the project team to digest in their own time.

Regardless of the size of the plan, it should be meaningful for the project team and stakeholders to follow. Some projects tend to break the plan into bite size chunks and obtain feedback from relevant streams to ensure accuracy. This can be a very time consuming task, but essential to the success of the project.

Waterfall Versus Agile

The two most popular methodologies for implementing procurement software that I have worked with are Waterfall, which might be more appropriately called the "classical" approach, and Agile, a specific type of Rapid Application Development.

From my experience either would work but I would tend to use a 'best of both' approach rather than focusing on one or the other. Both can be success in project world, but with technology and processes changing faster than ever, I would focus less on methodology and more on the organisational culture, innovation, goals and objectives.

In today's world, where process and technology has sell buy dates, you need to deploy methodologies that can accommodate changes with less impact on the project. My recommendation would be to adopt the structure of waterfall and the practicalities of agile to help deliver a procurement system.

In other words, still adopt the project phases and documentation during the solution design phase but start implementing solutions before the solution design phase has completed. By relaxing the rules but ensuring there is sufficient documentation for build means, you can safeguard any developments as part of the software lifecycle. Adopting a solely agile approach would mean that there may be no specifications, which can lead to risks when it comes to handover.

In a majority of the implementations that I have delivered it was impossible to run pure agile or pure waterfall due to many factors such as independent delivery of software without consulting dependent work streams or the project, third party involvement to deliver specific requirements such as interfaces, reliance on teams using the other methodology and overly complicated compliance. The project strategy should be in place to clearly define how implementations should be managed and delivered.

In summary, I would look to take some of the waterfall model structure and apply the principles of agile for rapid delivery. In the past, this has helped me deploy procurement projects successfully, on time and within budgets. In Step 4, I will discuss what areas of Waterfall versus Agile should be adopted in more details.

Project Step: High Level Design Strategies / Strategic Framework

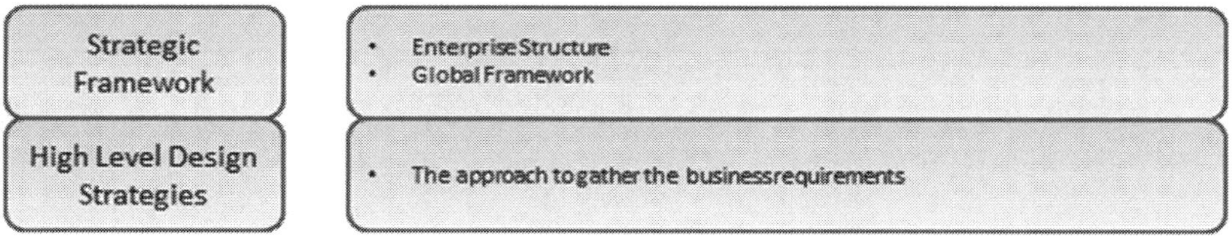

Strategic Framework	• Enterprise Structure • Global Framework
High Level Design Strategies	• The approach to gather the business requirements

This step explains two key areas that have helped me to successfully implement global procurement projects. The project strategy should have a section that explains how the high level design will be gathered along with global strategic elements.

High Level Design

When implementing procurement software and processes across multiple regions, I have found that trying to find common processes across many countries helps ensure a successful implement. Examples of this include:

- Global Contract Catalogues for all countries
- Common approach to Purchase to Receipt
- 80% - Common software design
- Simplified Approval Structures
- 20% - localisation based on legislation
- Streamlined procurement processes

The above is not always possible to achieve, but the strategic aim is to try and make it happen where possible. For a good template solution, anything above 80% common design is deemed a success. There will always be some localisations based on legal policies and work practices.

So, how can we streamline processes across large organisations? Well, it takes a lot of time, effort and requires stakeholders to manage the relationships across various regions. Kick off workshops and solution design walkthroughs should happen with various business representatives from each region to try and find ways to achieve the strategic objectives of the procurement strategy.

As previously mentioned, the strategic procurement goals should be based on the corporate strategy for the organisation, as a result the project strategy should also help achieve the procurement strategy achieve its objectives. Where applicable, common processes and approaches should be adopted and any deviations should be challenged. By evaluating the processes and size of each business units, exceptions may need to be built into the process to ensure procurement still works across the organisation.

Strategic Framework

The strategic framework is a detailed global standard across all areas of the software that is planned to be implemented. Large organisations benefit from implementing a strategic framework that could also be known as the Enterprise Structure because it outlines the fundamental areas.

Examples of this include:

- Legal Company Codes
- Various Numbering Conventions
- 2 way / 3 way match
- The Commodity Coding or Category Structure
- Purchase Order Numbering Conventions
- Thresholds for Financial Approval
- Chart of Accounts (CoA)
- Vendor Accounts
- Exchange Rate Types
- Various types of Master Data – Vendors, Budgets, Reporting

This is a detailed list and sometimes depends on the financial / procurement software application that is delivered. Having a repository (framework) in place helps the project understand the global standards and assess how to build the solution.

I have found this to be a useful exercise when implementing procurement solutions because it holds all the integration points that impact finance and procurement. I always refer back to the high level common design and strategic framework to understand what has been agreed.

In summary, as part of the project strategies, the high level design and strategic framework should be gathered during the solution design phase to support the project deliverables because it holds important data that is used to implement the software application.

Project Step: Implementation Partner

Implementation Partner

- Internal / External
- System Integrator

The final section within the project strategies step focuses on the implementation partner (IP) (also known as the system integrator (SI)). The majority of procurement implementations that I have worked on have been with implementation partners, consultancies that provide services to organisations such as IBM, KPMG, EY, Accenture et al.

When I speak to businesses about this particular area, it's interesting how each organisation has different approaches on how they select an implementation partner. I have tried to summarise some tips on how to select the right implementation partner below. In order to determine the right implementation partner for your organisation, simply evaluating the services they offer is not enough.

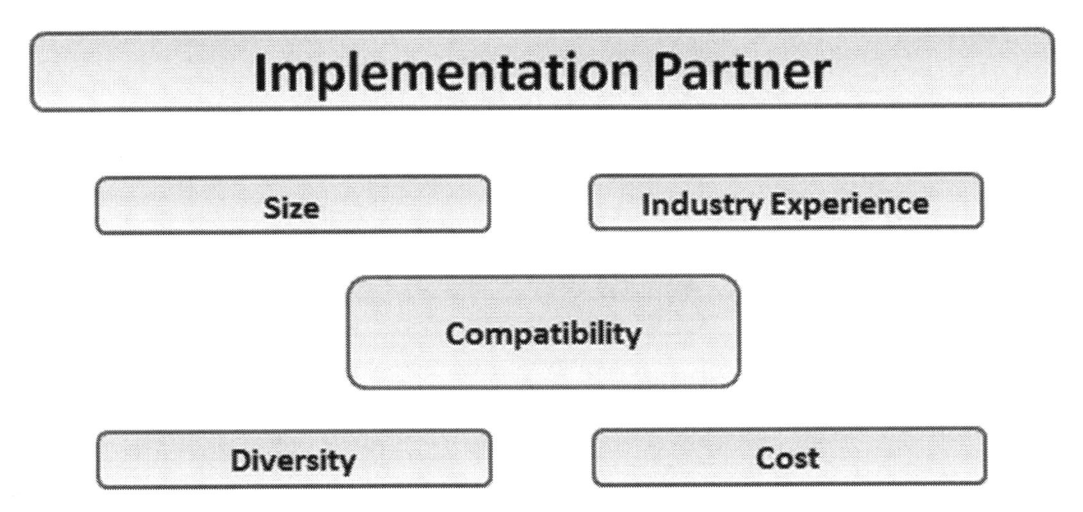

The above diagram demonstrates some key areas to evaluate when selecting an Implementation Partner.

Size

The size of the project is more important than the size of the IP. If you are implementing a large global project, you'll want an IP that has the bench strength to perform various areas of work, and that includes regional coverage in the countries to which you are deploying procurement.

Typically, smaller organisations look for IP's that exist for Small to Medium Enterprises (SME'S) as their budgets will be lower and the project size will also be less complex. Smaller IP's tend to bring highly experienced project teams with the same quality as larger IP's to ensure that the same level of service is provided to the organisation.

Experience with, and a track record for, similar implementations

You should also look to an IP that has the breadth of capabilities to help you drive this project. The larger consultancies are more likely to have the breadth and depth of capabilities to help with business process changes, programme management and change management, in addition to implementing the software. These are all areas discussed in this book and the likelihood is that the project will be a success based on the above factors.

Many of your processes and business requirements are specific to your industry, so it is important to benchmark and evaluate the IP on industrial experience. I worked for an IP that mainly concentrated on procurement systems for public sector organisations. The IP had a wealth of experience of implementing in this sector and, as a result, demonstrated the capability of delivering procurement solutions for other public sector organisations. Based on this factor, they were selected as the preferred vendor to deliver an upgrade for one of the public organisations I previously worked for.

Total cost of implementation

Some organisations I have worked with have gone with fixed price costs as part of implementations. I always seem to challenge this approach because every procurement project has its challenges and new requirements always arise half way through the project. If IP's quote fixed price rates, then anything new could cost them more and more money.

The importance is to ensure that you are comparing a like for like service from IP's. For example, it is not possible to compare a small to medium IP against a Big 4 in terms of cost, capability and culture.

Cultural Fit (Compatibility)

Another important factor is culture and compatibility. With organisations looking for a better brand and competitive advantage, they now expect innovative ways to implement unique processes that defines the business. Basically, you don't want to be treated like any other organisation and you don't want to be forced to adapt your processes and best practices to the software or vendor's methodology. Respect is important and the IP should understand how to manage the culture and work within the boundaries of it.

An IP should understand your business and replay that back to you in the form of a presentation. Finding a vendor that respects the qualities that have made your organisation successful is crucial to implementing a system that will support continued success.

The type of implementation should also be considered when selecting an IP. I have implemented procurement systems where there was just a technical upgrade of a procurement system with very few process improvements. If an upgrade is purely technical, you should look for a partner that has the tools and methodology to implement at a low cost and with little disruption to the organisation and business processes.

The other extreme is if the project is wider and impacts the whole of finance. In this case the specialist project teams will be required to process harmonisation initiatives with cross-functional teams that can bring business process best practices, strong programme management disciplines and change management capabilities and software exposure.

One key tip that I would like to share with you is not to look to award parts of a project to multiple implementation partners. I have worked on a couple of projects where the Solution Design (blueprinting phase) was awarded to a Big 4 consultancy and the actual build to another implementation partner. The common goal was to get the two parties to work together and ensure the project was delivered based on the business requirements. With the added complexity of the offshore model to resource the delivery phases of the project, the whole process of implementing a global solution became very challenging and time consuming. I would recommend selecting an implementation partner based on the key evaluation criteria described in this Step 3.

In summary, there is no denying that choosing an implementation partner is a decision which must be taken with some caution and can be quite concerning. For those that have never experienced the need to evaluate implementation partners, the volume of information to assess can become overwhelming and sometimes repetitive. Decision making can divide us all when cost, cultural fit, previous experience, industrial experience and resources are presented by the implementation partners.

I have also observed that some implementation partners are awarded projects based on previous relationships between senior management and IP's. Trust and understanding is also a very important factor in the selection process.

STEP 4

PROJECT LIFE CYCLE

STEP 4 – Project life cycle (Software)

Summary of Step 4:

When it comes to delivery of procurement projects, the life cycle is very important. Clearly defined practices on how to rapidly implement processes without risking project delivery is very important to the success.

The solution design phase should be managed and appropriate resources assigned to ensure that all areas of procurement are identified and requirements gathered accurately. Some projects I have implemented were not as successful as they could have been because the requirements were not very clear and the delivered solution did not satisfy the customer expectations.

In this step, collaboration is priceless to the delivery of a successful procurement system. The SME's, Functional Teams and BA's should work together along with other teams to ensure end to end processes are understood and delivered. It is more often that I observe teams working in their own space and fail to understand the integration with each other. This causes issues later in the project phases when gaps are identified during testing phases.

This section will discuss the software development life cycle (SDLC) in more detail. The diagram below demonstrates a comprehensive list of steps that are executed before the project is physically started.

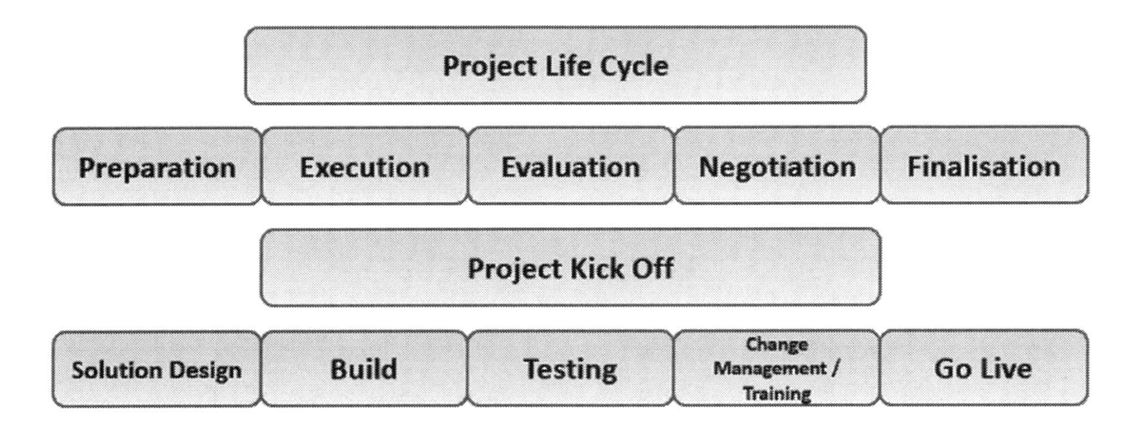

The prerequisite steps include:

- Identify stakeholders and obtain their acceptance
- Identify business needs
- Identify high level options
- Identify lessons learned from previous / similar projects
- Prepare project summary and initiate project initiation (PID)
- Project Evaluation
- Resolve any option points from project evaluation

- Agree next steps from Project Evaluation
- Approval of strategic solution and budget sign off in principle
- Completion of Business Justification

- Outline Design
- Select Implementation Partner
- Approve Resources
- Finalise budgets

- Create Project Plan
- Identify Business Resources
- Identify Project Management Methodology
- Identify Software Lifecycle
- Project Kick Off

The above is a list of key steps, but each organisation will may have additional steps that require completing.

There are 6 project phases, each with identifiable roles & responsibilities.

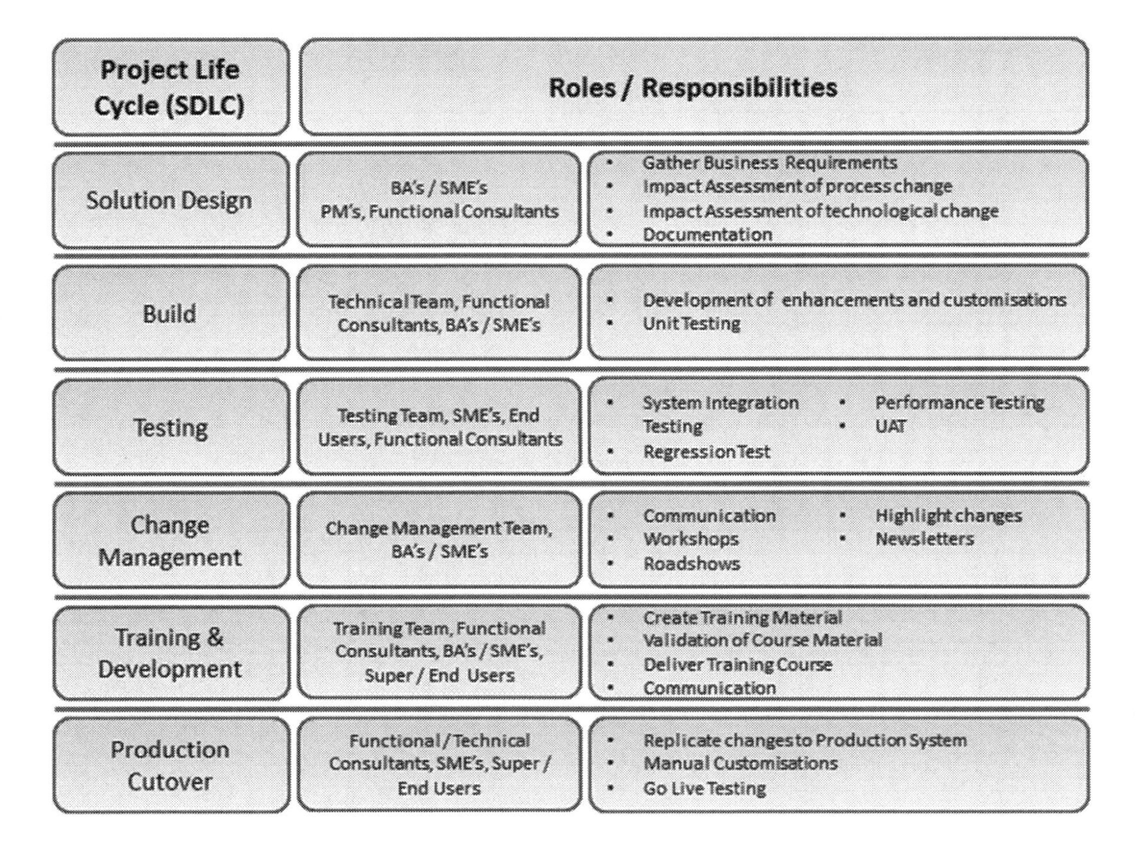

Let's look at each phase in detail to understand how each phase can contribute to the successful implementation of a procurement system.

From my experience the main phases that make up a typical procurement software life cycle include:

- Phase 1: Solution Design
- Phase 2: Build
- Phase 3: Test
- Phase 4: Change Management
- Phase 5: Training & Development
- Phase 6: Production Cutover / Go Live

In order to deliver the software within the timescales and within budget, the methodology I would adopt is a hybrid model of Waterfall and Agile. Typically this means start solution design as soon as the requirements are documented, start prototyping and building solutions (Phase 1 and 2) and demonstrate solutions to the business as and when built. Also, Change Management should start engagement earlier rather than later and create material that will be useful to the business.

Indeed, business engagement is very important and should be conducted at all levels of the organisation from stakeholder, super user and to the end user community.

Project Life Cycle Step: Solution Design

Solution Design	BA's / SME's PM's, Functional Consultants	• Gather Business Requirements • Impact Assessment of process change • Impact Assessment of technological change • Documentation

The solution design project phase is ensuring the requirements have been gathered accurately and involves the completion of the blueprinting phase. This phase can be broken down into two sub-phases.

- **High Level Solution Design**
  - Agree on the scope of S2P areas to be implemented
  - Identify processes to be improved and impacted
  - Understand the high level as-is processes
  - Understand the high level to-be processes
  - Understand the People and how Technology will be adopted
  - Understand the to-be integrated business processes
  - Document the High Level Solution Design
  - Workshops to understand all of the above
  - Sign Off from business representatives, Business Process Owners (BPO's), SME's and BA's
- **Detailed Solution Design**
  - Deep dive into the process areas, for example Contract Management, Master Data, Purchase Requests, Approvals, Catalogues, Purchase Orders and Confirmations
  - Gather additional requirements based on specific procurement areas
  - Document all requirements into a detailed design document
  - Analyse requirements against software capability
  - Generate a list of enhancements in the form of a WRICEF (Workflow, Reports, Interfaces, Customisations, Enhancements, Forms) List

- Workshops to replay requirements and obtain acceptance from all
- Create Functional Specifications on the finalised requirements based on the list of enhancements identified
- Prototype solutions to demonstrate capability of software capability based on standard functionality
- Sign off detailed design documentation
- Sign off functional specifications

Once the high level design phase has been completed, it is advantageous to demonstrate the standard software to the business representatives, so they can assess the as-is and to-be processes and visualise any requirements and changes. This will also be helpful for the change management team as they start to build a repository of differences and impacts to the user community.

The solution design phase can take up to 3 months to complete depending on the scope of the software implementation and involves a number of check points to evaluate the processes. As we are looking to implement agile ways of working, there must still be enough detail in the functional specification to start building solutions. Hard sign off of solution design can take many weeks and it's important to start building as soon as possible.

Process Owners for each stream should take responsibility of their areas to ensure they understand and give sign off on documentation as soon as possible. Demonstrates should help with the sign off process. BA's and SME's could also report back to Process Owners on any decisions that impact their areas.

Project Life Cycle Step: Build

Build	Technical Team, Functional Consultants, BA's / SME's	• Development of enhancements and customisations • Unit Testing • Documentation • Functional Testing

The build project phase is about setting up the software to work with the organisation. This includes standard customisations, development work for any WRICEF objects based on completed functional specifications, prototyping, investigation and analysis of requirements and environmental issues with the software client.

I always find it beneficial to work closely with the build team during a project and ensure the designed solution is developed using innovative ways. The build team cannot always build solutions based on functional specifications because they may not understand the requirements and roadmap, as they were not part of the solution design phase.

If organisations want to deploy solutions that are robust and clear, the functional and technical teams should work together. Also, from a development team perspective, it is advantageous if the same technical consultants work on S2P enhancements as they can think of consistent approaches and coding.

I always ensure that functional specifications are updated with the finalised design and technical details. This helps when handing over to the support team post go live. The development team should also complete technical documentation as part to their role once a WRICEF object has been fully completed.

Project Life Cycle Step: Testing

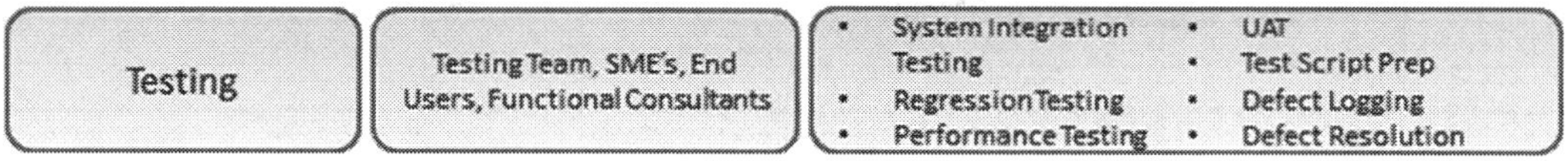

Testing	Testing Team, SME's, End Users, Functional Consultants	• System Integration Testing • Regression Testing • Performance Testing • UAT • Test Script Prep • Defect Logging • Defect Resolution

The testing phase is very important for the success of a procurement system because it helps identify how the processes are integrated together and reduces the risks when users start processing transactions post deployment. Whenever I implement a procurement process, I always spend a considerable amount of time testing the processes and technology before handing over to the business teams. It is important to define test scope and testing scenarios before carrying out any testing.

Sign off from the business is also required, but does not need to be done before testing has started. Functional Specifications should also have a section in testing scenarios and this should be used as a basis to test functional enhancements.

The various testing phases that typically benefit the success of procurement systems include:

Unit Testing

Testing enhancements and customisations in small chunks and completed by the technical team is a definition of unit testing. A good example is when enhancing the procurement system with validations based on business conditions to prevent users from doing things they should not be allowed to do when processing procurement transactions. When requesting a PO, the user should not be able to approve requests that they have created as this should only be processed by an approver.

Functional Testing

Functional Testing is based on customisations / enhancements and should cover off business requirements and be executed by functional consultants. A good example is to test the functional specifications based on business scenarios and also execute negative testing to ensure that the enhancements work without loopholes.

System Integration Testing

Testing customised and enhancements against business requirements, including integration with finance. This phase of testing is very important and overlaps with functional testing. It looks at both business related scenarios and is integrated with finance and other related areas. This is the first time where full end to end integration is tested. A good example is when testing the Purchase to Receipt process with Invoice Processing. Some test steps include:

1. Create Purchase Request
2. Approvals
3. PO Creation
4. PO Confirmation
5. Invoice Creation
6. Invoice Matching
7. Invoice Payment to Supplier

It is always beneficial to start testing of this phase as soon as possible. The sooner any defects are highlighted, the better chance you have for a successful procurement implementation.

User Acceptance Testing

User Acceptance Testing (UAT) is one of the last phases of the software testing process. During UAT, the user community test the software to make sure it can handle required tasks in real-world scenarios, according to specifications. This is normally end to end testing with integration with other areas.

For the UAT phase to be a success, the UAT testing phase requires good management and full business engagement. I often find project teams underestimate the preparation that should be done before executing UAT testing and I have highlighted some considerations:

1. Agreement Scope of UAT Testing – I would recommend testing the most frequent scenarios and critical processes
2. Create Test Scripts and sign off from the business before the start of testing
3. Prepare software application for testing
4. Identify the user community that will participate in UAT
5. Run through training with the user community
6. Identify defect management processes
7. Sign off process to approve completed UAT
8. Identify exit criteria for UAT

As you can see, there are a lot of activities that take place before UAT actually starts. The above has worked successfully for me when managing UAT. A testing manager can help manage the above steps.

Based on the culture, ensure that UAT takes place in comfortable surroundings and, before UAT begins, run through some basic processes to ensure that the process and technology work as desired. I normally run a few test scripts with multiple scenarios to help ensure that UAT is a success.

Performance Testing

Performance Testing is testing the quality of the system including reliability, responsiveness, stability and technical resources. This form of testing is not always easy to execute when implementing new procurement systems and processes but should be relatively easy to identify when upgrading from one version to another.

Performance testing is becoming widely adopted by many organisations in today's world as there is more reliance of technology to help run business processes. Assumptions are made on what is deemed acceptable and the scope is generally to ensure that the system works in situations such as having 100 concurrent users on the system performing various activities.

Regression Testing

Regression testing is one which verifies that software, which was previously developed and tested, still performs correctly after it was changed. Changes may include software enhancements, patches, configuration changes, etc.

This step becomes very important when changes have been made to functions and processes that have previously been tested and passed. I have found the following useful:

1. Identify scope of regression testing based on changes implemented
2. Agree with business, the regression testing scope
3. Utilise test scripts from previous testing phases as a baseline
4. Prepare data to allow testing to take place
5. Workshops to understand changes
6. Impact assessment of changes and agree regression testing

I always try and test all functionality during all the testing cycles to give the business confidence and reassurance that there is low impact to the technology and processes. This is not always possible, in which case try and cover multiple scenarios during the regression testing phase.

Project Life Cycle Step: Change Management

Change Management	Change Management Team, BA's / SME's	• Communication • Workshops • Roadshows • Highlight changes • Newsletters

Another key area from a people and process perspective is change management. If change management is incorrectly managed, there could be a chance that the procurement system could fail. The key is to manage change in a positive and constructive manner.

Many organisations spend time implementing change management processes but I would look to internal business members to help support this area. Building relationships with key areas and stakeholders is very important to ensure everyone is on the same page and understanding.

A key aspect of the change management process is to evaluate the transformation and impacts to people, process and technology. Understand the current and evaluate against the imminent processes, consider how the new software application fits against current and future processes.

Highlighting the main changes as part of the implementation journey can help ensure the business understands that change is coming. Roadshows, presentations, solution walkthroughs and newsletters can all help the resistance to change. More will be discussed in Step 5.

The key to a successful procurement system is for the project team to work positively with change management to aid them to understand changes to processes, technology and people and to then promote the project and processes.

Project Life Cycle Step: Training & Development

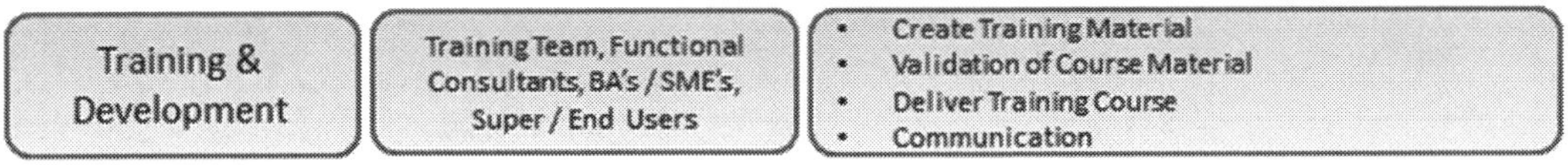

Training & Development	Training Team, Functional Consultants, BA's / SME's, Super / End Users	• Create Training Material • Validation of Course Material • Deliver Training Course • Communication

Training & Development is important for procurement implementations because if people don't understand the business process (changes) and how they integrate with their day to day business role, then purchasing can be a very long-winded and complex process.

I have worked on projects where training and development was managed brilliantly because of the level of engagement involved in the business writing the training material and with the collaboration to deliver training to the user community. This was beneficial to the project because the delivery of the training was given by SME's and super users who understand the end to end business processes.

Technology can only be delivered appropriately if the training material has the right content. I have worked on projects where most training was delivered via simulations and e-learning material, which caused confusion and lack of understanding. E-learning is great but should be used for smaller projects where the impact is not very big or on subjects that do not cause any confusion.

Choosing who to train is also important. I would suggest all users that will have access to the new system should be given the opportunity to attend a training course. Some organisations only train frequent users which can be dangerous as training will then need to be given post go live to the rest of the team. It can also give the user community a negative mind set because they will not have understood the change in processes and technology.

A training strategy should always be in the project plan and it should also describe how, when, where, method of training and volume of users that will be trained. The timing of when the training takes place should be in line with when go-live is planned. There is no point training users 6 weeks before go live. Any changes to go-live dates will have an impact on end user training. Some organisations have a separate training team to deliver training and others that I have worked with utilise functional consultants and SME's / BA's to deliver the training.

Project Life Cycle Step: Production Cutover

Production Cutover	Functional / Technical Consultants, SME's, Super / End Users	• Replicate changes to Production System • Manual Customisations • Go Live Testing

The final step of the project life cycle is to do with cutover and go-live. It is important to point out, when you get to this phase of the project, a series of sign offs would take place and an exit criteria with a check list would have been agreed and approved.

Of course, UAT results will have a lot to do with it along with what support models need to be in place post cutover. Some projects tend to have a technical cutover followed by a business cutover a week or two later. This reduces the risk of things going wrong and gives the project a chance to fix them before effecting business operations.

I would always favour a technical cutover first (if this is possible). If this is not an option, then trial/rehearsal cutovers should prove that the actual cutover will be a success. Cutover itself can be reasonably straightforward if planned, managed and communicated accordingly. I have worked on projects where cutovers have been successful and others where cutover has been a little more difficult, but still a success in the end.

The complexity depends on the size and scope of the project. If the procurement project is for a small area, with limited enhancements and manual steps post cutover, the likelihood is that cutover will be a success. If the project relates to procurement, finance and reporting going live at once, then it is more complicated as there are dependencies on each other because of the integrated points.

A good example of this is master data. If master data has not been uploaded (migrated), then the procurement system may not be able to transfer them into their systems and follow-on dependencies such as contracts and catalogues cannot be set up.

The success of an implementation can also be measured on the cutover being completed correctly. User accounts set up, customised data set up, default settings and so on. I have experienced projects where cutover does not go to plan and user accounts were given incorrect privileges, which meant they could not access the system.

To avoid issues during and post cutover, the support model and hyper care processes should be identified and communicated to all. This should be extended to the user community and stakeholders.

Super user involvement is always beneficial as they can give personal attention and log incidents where appropriate. The more hands that are available and visible, the better it is for the project. First impressions always count and if the user community feels that issues are not addressed and resolved in time, the project can be deemed a failure. Perception is the key and this must be managed by the project.

The main tasks that are involved in the production cutover phase include:

- Exit Criteria / Business Readiness Checks
- Go, No Go Decision post cutover
- Cutover Plan, dependencies, functional, technical tasks
- Identification of Business Resource for post cutover testing
- Communication
- Actual Cutover
- Go Live Support
- Handing over to Support (Post Hyper Care)

In summary, the production cutover phase is the final piece of the jigsaw and involves the majority of the project and business teams to push the project live. Again, it is important to remain positive as well as support the post go live system defects.

From my experience, I have included my top tips for working positively during project lifecycle steps below.

Solution Design Phase

- Close open design decisions as early as possible
- Group similar requirements into same Functional Documents to help accelerate development
- Ensure interfaces are identified in order for them to be implemented in a uniformed way
- Engage technical and functional teams as early as possible to accelerate developments

Build Phase

- Collaboration between technical and functional teams
- Invest in technical tools to automate processes
- Ensure project teams have the right access to do customisations and developments

Testing Phase

- Test and Practice the support processes. This will enhance better results during cutover due to the multiple testing phasing.

Cutover / Hyper Care (Post Go Live Support)

- Don't allow mass changes in the 2 weeks before cutover
- A dedicated cutover manager is essential and should not be deemed a part time role
- Manual releases are time consuming – due to this the rehearsal of cutover becomes a very laborious task
- Test all sites for firewall issues before going live
- Client access (user access from all locations)
- User/project access in production systems

- Consultant roles should be identified before go live
- Support Model should be agreed and in place
- Ensure daily reports are in place to monitor ownership, progress and trends

Project Management

- Everlasting change... the scope of the functional / technical build workload needs greater attention and management
- This causes additional development and testing effort – but also re-planning effort for leads and PMO
- For reporting and daily work management you need a tool that manages the WRICEF catalogue
- MS Project can't do it all
- A simple rule helps – if it's assigned to you, then you have the next action on that WRICEF
- Do not use spread sheets as they can be time consuming and are limited in their usefulness
- Collaboration tools are very helpful otherwise it forces people to use emails – the worst tool for fostering team work
- Email discussions should be banned as they are counter-productive
- Instead, use forums – at least the comments and decisions become an asset to the project, rather than being hidden
- When analysing the time lost fiddling with audio/video, bad network connections – it would be easy to justify the cost of better facilities

For more information, contact Revolution Global Services Limited via email Nadeem.Surve1@gmail.com.

STEP 5

CHANGE MANAGEMENT

STEP 5 – Change management

Summary of Step 5:

The final piece of the jigsaw is the change management area. Regardless of the other 4 steps, if people, process and technology is not understood and managed efficiently, your project could be deemed a failure.

Transition, communication, training and development must all be managed and delivered to all concerned parties in a clear and concise way, to help them understand what is about to come. The current, transition and future states should be managed through the appropriate methods and the change management team should listen to the organisation.

Culture, style and presentation methods should be evaluated before delivering any communication pieces to the organisations. I have often observed email communication being sent to all users because it is easy, fast and efficient, but it is not always effective if the culture of the business is to delete it or misunderstand it. Newsletters, intranet pages, roadshows, super user involvement could be more effective to deliver the message.

The final step in the 5 step process is change management. This step is very important to the success of a procurement system, especially if processes are changed and software applications are transferred from one system to another. I have worked with many organisations where change management effectively helps the business both understand change and avoids resistance to it.

Definition

Change management (CM) refers to any approach to transitioning individuals, teams, and organizations using methods intended to re-direct the use of resources, business process, budget allocations, or other modes of operation that significantly reshape a company or organization (from Wikipedia).

Change Management

People

Process

Training and Development

Technology

Communication

Effective change management takes into consideration people, process and technology but is not limited to these areas. As part of this step, we will also discuss training and development processes.

Process Step: People (Organisation)

The first process step I want to highlight is the people element. When implementing procurement systems, people are very important. They are involved in all areas of procurement from Source to Award to Invoice Processing. Technology is now making the people element focus on other aspects of procurement (negotiations with suppliers), analysing and evaluating of supplier performance and analysis of spend.

Organisational Change can also be a very sensitive subject when automation replaces the dependency on people. I have noticed a huge shift in procurement organisational change, mainly in the areas of purchase to receipt. Most organisations now adopt a self-service approach to raising purchase requests. Departmental buying is becoming obsolete and, with simple, easy to follow online purchasing tools, self-service seems to be the way forward. This gives the operational procurement team opportunities to focus on relationships with suppliers.

When looking at big transformation projects, organisational change can have a very big impact. Change must be realistic, achievable and measurable.

These aspects are especially relevant to managing personal change. The steps that require attention include:

- Evaluation organisational change
- Identify key elements to focus on
- Communication Strategy to project, employees, stakeholders

Organisational change will be more effective if you apply simple principles. Change management entails planning and sensitive implementation, consultation with, and involvement of, the people affected by the changes. Experience has shown if change is forced upon people, this normally causes problems. Before starting organisational change, you need to ask yourself the following:

- What is the objective of this change?
- How to assess change has been achieved?
- Who is affected by this change, and how will they react to it?
- How much of this change can change management help support?
- How do we get a positive feel from the business?

Some tips from experience include:

- Do not 'sell' change in workshops / walkthroughs, instead let the organisation understand change and ask questions
- Understand the culture and type of organisation and adapt accordingly, do not force change by not talking their language
- Check that people understand change or at least agree to the need for change and explain how the change will be managed
- Encourage stakeholders to talk to their employees before change management has meetings with them
- Communicate change in a positive manner

Process Step: Process

Along with people, process changes should be identified, communicated and demonstrates in the right manner. For smaller organisations, this can be delivered by small workshops or during the training sessions. For larger procurement projects, a change management team could be in place to manage, identify process change by discussing with the project team.

The principles for change should include:

- Involve and agree support from people within organisation
- Communicate, involve, enable and facilitate involvement from people, as early and openly and as fully as is possible.
- Take into account system related to process changes
- Cultural aspects of related to process change
- Behaviours and personal perceptions.

When looking into process in more detail, you should look at where you are today (current), where you want to go (future) and how you will get there (transition).

The three states of change provide a way to demonstrate how change actually occurs. Whether the change is an Enterprise Resource Planning application, or business process improvements, there is always a Current State (how things are done today), a Future State (how things will be done) and a Transition State (how to move from A to B).

Current Processes (As-Is)

- Identify current processes, behaviours and organisational structures
- Identify job roles that makes the current process work
- Understand current processes and how they operate

Based on the above, evaluation criteria should be created to measure the level of change against the to-be process.

Future Processes (To-Be)

The Future State is where we are trying to get to. In projects that I have implemented, this is not often fully defined and can actually shift during the project phases. The aim of the Future State is to be better than the Current State in terms of performance and efficiency. The Future State may not match our professional goals, and there is a chance that we may not be successful in the Future State. This should be made clear in any workshops, walkthroughs and meetings that are held with the business.

Transition (How to make it happen)

This phase can be disorganised and involves a lot of collaboration with the project team and the organisation. It requires coordination to gather all the relevant information, job to role mapping, roles and authorisations, understanding how to bring change and keep everyone in the loop.

Some organisations use the ADKAR 5 step process to manage change.

- **Awareness** of the need for change
- **Desire** to participate and support the change
- **Knowledge** on how to change
- **Ability** to implement the required skills and behaviours
- **Reinforcement** to sustain the change

Managing change as a process from the organisational view helps to ensure that the right activities are occurring at the right time, and that employees are receiving the right information they need to move through their own personal process of change.

Process Step: Training and Development

For change to be successful it can sometimes rely on how the training material is created and delivered. As an experienced trainer, I always try and explain the people, process and technology elements with simple to follow process flows. My delivery style is to use innovative methods to deliver training and course material.

The last thing I would want is to confuse the user community. I have observed some training methods that have confused the user community because of the delivery methods adopted. Things to consider when creating training material and delivering training include:

- The training material must highlight the current and future state
- The training material should clearly highlight the people, process and technology
- The training material should have a section on acronyms / glossary
- The training material should have step by step scenarios
- Quick Reference Guides should be created to help infrequent users
- Where possible, ensure there is a subject matter expert available to answer any business related questions
- When delivering training courses, interact in a positive manner
- When delivering training courses, be enthusiastic, willing to answer questions and take into account behaviours and culture
- A training plan is a good way to manage training schedules and course information

In summary, training and development must be deployed with good organisation and management. The course material should be approved by the SME's and business before delivery. Trainers should work closely with functional consultants, SME's and Business Analysts to ensure the information is accurate and easy to follow.

Process Step: Communication

With any change management process, communicate is very important. A communications plan should be created and content of an effective communications plan parallels or matches where employees are in the process of change. Early communication efforts (set the scene) should focus on explaining the Current State and why it does not work and reasons why it must be changed. Communications later on in the change process can begin to focus on details (transition) and the eventual results the project or initiative is aiming to deliver. Too much information about the complete picture with unknowns can sometimes cause confusion and more unanswered questions raised by the business. Always ensure first communications to employees provides vision of the change and keep it simple so there is no ambiguity.

Consider employee's feelings, culture, behaviours and remember to interact with them and obtain their acceptance by positivity. I generally start with a kick off session and explain the aim and objective of the session. Scan around the room and run through the agenda and try to understand behaviours through body language.

If you would like case studies or more information, contact Revolution Global Services Limited via email Nadeem.Surve1@gmail.com.

SUMMARY

Summary

This book has tried to cover a number of topics to help organisations, procurement professionals and those who would like a career in procurement understand the complexities involved when implementing a procurement system. As you go through the various topics and understand the procurement lifecycle, it is clear that procurement has many elements and is a very important part of the corporate strategy for businesses.

Procurement strategy is very important to organisations as it feeds into the overall business strategy. Businesses must identify how they plan to analyse spend, report on vendor performance and create a procurement roadmap in terms of a centralised procurement function across all business areas or regional and local depending on categories of spend.

The 10 helpful tips in the book should help readers understand how to successfully implement a procurement system. The tips are summarised below:

TIP 1 – Scope of Procurement Process

TIP 2 – The importance of Software Selection

TIP 3 – Adopt the appropriate Project Management Methods

TIP 4 – Invest in Change Management

TIP 5 – Select the right Implementation Partner

TIP 6 – Invest the right amount of time in the Planning

TIP 7 – Identify Roles and Responsibilities

TIP 8 – Communication Channels

TIP 9 – Focus on the value of Procurement and not just the Cost

TIP 10 – Collaboration

Also, the 5 step approach should give readers an understanding of the implications to get it right in order to implement a successful procurement system. The steps included the below:

Step 1: Procurement Strategy

Step 2: Procurement Roadmap

Step 3: Project Strategies

Step 4: Project Life Cycle

Step 5: Change Management

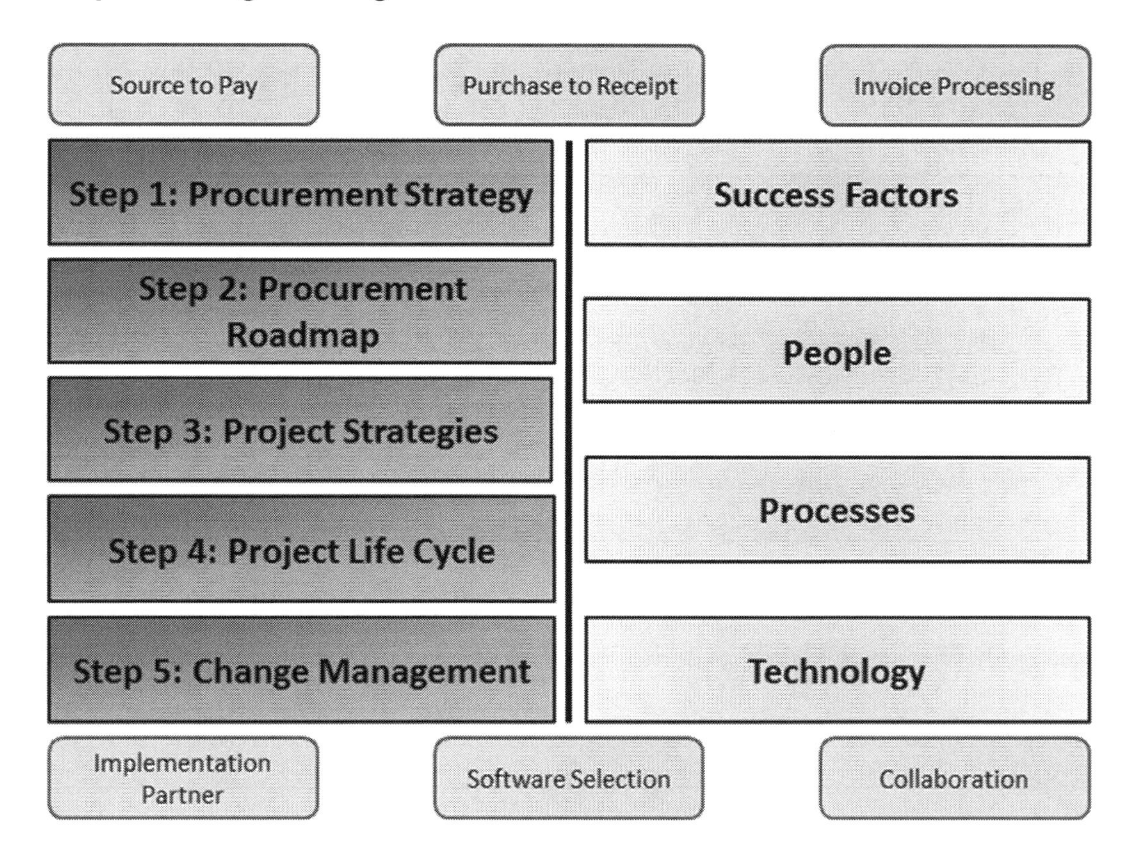

Let's summarise the key points from this book.

Step 1: Procurement Strategy

As the world of procurement is changing rapidly, it is important that the procurement strategy also has the vision and capabilities to evolve. It must take into account organisation, processes and technology along with ensuring it fulfils the corporate goals set by the organisation.

Finally, the procurement strategy should be systematic, look at the long term goals and take on a holistic approach to ensure it stays ahead of the market.

Step 2: Procurement Roadmap

The procurement roadmap was the next step in the process and looked at the importance of various aspects within procurement. It started with the Strategic elements, whereby suppliers are enabled via the source to award process, then talked about how the award is operationally procured using the purchase to receipt processes and finally explained how suppliers were paid via the invoice processing element.

The procurement roadmap is very important to the success of procurement systems because it starts with evaluation of vendors that could be awarded a contract based on a requirement and ends with the supplier eventually getting payment for goods and services.

The key point is to define the requirement as clearly as possible, before entering into any tendering processes. Most businesses tend to give opportunities to suppliers they currently work with to build stronger relationships and obtain better services with them.

Step 3: Project Strategies

There are a number of processes that take place within the project strategies process area. Before a project is started, a PID needs is created which involves a business case and various evaluations completed. What problem are you trying to resolve? What type of return on investment (ROI) do you expect? What does the project delivery look like in terms of resource, communication and timeframes?

These are typical questions that need answering and, also, does the project strategy complement the corporate goals of the organisation? There are examples of various resourcing models for small and large projects.

The project management methodology has an impact on the outcome of a procurement system. I tend to use a hybrid of Waterfall / Agile and many organisations where I have implemented software seem to adopt the same.

Step 4: Project Life Cycle

When it comes to delivery of procurement projects, the life cycle is very important. Clearly defined practices on how to rapidly implement processes without risking project delivery are very key to the success.

The solution design phase should be managed and appropriate resources assigned to ensure that all areas of procurement are identified and requirements gathered accurately. Some projects I have implemented were not as successful as they could have been because the requirements were not very clear and the delivered solution did not satisfy the customer expectations.

In this step, collaboration is priceless to the delivery of a successful procurement system. The SME's, Functional Teams and BA's should work together along with other teams to ensure end to end processes are understood and delivered. It is more often that I observe teams working in their own space and fail to understand the integration with each other. This causes issues later in the project phases when gaps are identified during testing phases.

Step 5: Change Management

The final piece of the jigsaw is the change management area. Regardless of the other 4 steps, if people, process and technology is not understood and managed efficiently, your project could be deemed a failure.

Transition, communication, training and development must all be managed and delivered to all concerned parties in a clear and concise way, to help them understand what is about to come. The current, transition and future states should be managed through the appropriate methods and the change management team should listen to the organisation.

Culture, style and presentation methods should be evaluated before delivering any communication pieces to the organisations. I have often observed email communication being sent to all users because it is easy, fast and efficient, but it is not always effective if the culture of the business is to delete it or misunderstand it. Newsletters, intranet pages, roadshows, super user involvement could be more effective to deliver the message.

As a final statement, as you have experienced by reading this book, procurement is complicated and the 5 steps explained in this book is to guide the reader through the complex journey of procurement and to try and simplify things when implementing people, process and technology to help ensure a successfully implementation of a procurement system.

If you require consulting advice, workshops, walkthroughs, please contact Revolution Global Services Limited via email Nadeem.Surve1@gmail.com.

AUTHOR INFORMATION

Author Information

Please find contact information for the author below:

1. **LinkedIn Profile**

https://uk.linkedin.com/in/nadeem-surve-28b61a2

2. **Facebook Author Page**

https://www.facebook.com/NadeemSurveAuthor

3. **Amazon Author Page**

https://www.amazon.co.uk/-/e/B071196FL2

4. **For management consultancy, workshops, advice, training & development, please contact Revolution Global Services Limited via email** Nadeem.Surve1@gmail.com

Made in the USA
Middletown, DE
28 February 2022